T0193515

SPIES
IN PALESTINE

••••••••••••••••••••••

Love, Betrayal, and the Heroic
Life of Sarah Aaronsohn

JAMES SRODES

COUNTERPOINT
Berkeley

Library of Congress Cataloging-in-Publication Data
Names: Srodes, James, author.
Title: Spies in Palestine : love, betrayal, and the heroic life of Sarah
  Aaronsohn / James Srodes.
Description: Berkeley, CA : Counterpoint Press, [2016] | Includes
  bibliographical references and index.
Identifiers: LCCN 2016040205 | ISBN 9781619026131 (alk. paper)
Subjects: LCSH: Aaronsohn, Sarah. | Aaronson family. | Aaronsohn, Aaron,
  1876-1919. | NILI (Organization : Palestine) |
  Zionists--Palestine--Biography.
Classification: LCC DS125.3.A864 S66 2016 | DDC 940.4/865694092 [B] --dc23
LC record available at https://lccn.loc.gov/2016040205

ISBN 978-1-64009-005-7

Cover design by Kelly Winton
Interior design by Tabitha Lahr

Photographs courtesy of the Beit Aaronsohn Museum, Zichron Ya'akove, Israel

COUNTERPOINT
2560 Ninth Street, Suite 318
Berkeley, CA 94710
www.counterpointpress.com

Printed in the United States of America

For Cecile
My Love Endures

CONTENTS

AUTHOR'S NOTE

Twenty years ago I was deep in the files of what was then known as the British Public Records Office, now their National Archives, in the London suburb of Kew. As part of my research for a biography of Allen W. Dulles, the architect of and longest-serving director of the U.S. Central Intelligence Agency, I was looking through pre–World War I records for the first reference British intelligence service had for Dulles at the start of his lifelong career as a spy.

While British historical records are among the most meticulous, every archive has occasional documents that end up misfiled. To my surprise I found such a misplaced document. It was what was called a "minute," dated 1920, a memorandum that circulated among various government agencies. In those glory days of the Empire's bureaucracy, a "minute" was a large yellow document, fully eighteen by twelve inches, that had a three-inch space the length of the left-hand side where relevant civil servants had to sign their initials showing they had read it, as well as providing space for them to comment.

This document had started with the War Office, then been approved by the Foreign Office, and was finally emerging from the British Treasury for action. It appropriated ten thousand pounds (hundreds of thousands of today's dollars) to be spent by the British High Commission that ruled postwar Palestine to rebuild an agricultural experiment station at a coastal village called Athlit. It noted that the Turkish Army had destroyed the station in the waning days of World War I in reprisal against the Palestinian Jews who had operated the station and who had provided intelligence vital to the British victory in that region.

What caught my eye was a handwritten comment in the margins by one of the civil servants who had passed on the minute. It said, "Considering our moral responsibility for the unhappy fate of the 'A Organization,' this is the least we could do." At a time when the British Empire's servants recognized few moral imperatives other than the advancement of the British flag and British commerce, this struck me as odd and so I made a note of it, put it away, and forgot about it.

As often happens, this first sighting of the "A Organization" led to other references over the years and brought me to the story of Sarah Aaronsohn, the remarkable young woman who put her life in peril to direct a spy operation that led to a dramatic British victory over the Ottoman allies of Germany's Kaiser. Part of the story that seized my imagination was the back story of how in those earliest days of the return of Jews from Europe to their Biblical homeland, there was a brief window of opportunity for a peaceful alliance of mutual interests with their indigenous Arab neighbors. Like most true stories, it is one of romance and loss as well as triumph, that is richer than any fictional tale. In Sarah's story we also see choices being made that set in motion the sad events we see in that unhappy region today.

Every biographer stands on the shoulders of the writers who went before him. I am no exception and freely thank the authors of the many histories of the First World War fought in the Middle East and of the lives of the principal characters—the Aaronsohn family, T.E. Lawrence, the Ottoman rulers, and the British and American political figures who groped through the fog of war and national ambitions.

It is an important caution for the reader that not all histories, and certainly not all biographies, on this topic are in agreement. Contradictions of fact, disagreements over interpretation, and individual motives of the historians themselves can confuse. One of the tantalizing puzzles of the Sarah Aaronsohn story is the widely believed romance with T.E. Lawrence—the fabled Lawrence of Arabia. Lawrence himself may have believed it was so. My task then was to navigate through these contradictions, mix in my new research, and apply my own interpretation of a vastly different time and people and tell the best story of Sarah Aaronsohn's life that I could.

—James Srodes
Washington, DC
May 2016

PROLOGUE

A Knock at the Door

•••••••••••••••••••••••••

October 2–9, 1917

For the Jews settled along the Mediterranean shores of the
land known as Syria–Palestine, the final days of September
1917 should have been a time of plentiful harvests, family cel-
ebrations, and the sustaining observances of the season's important religious holidays. But not in 1917. The once unimaginable
carnage of the Great War was entering its third year with no
end in sight. Too soon the war that began in 1914 turned to
no purpose except to impel more young lives into the maw of
a monstrous killing machine that stretched from France to the
Arabian Gulf.

Now after two years of starvation, there was a new threat
of a genocidal pogrom by the Ottoman Turkish government.
Many of those settlers who had clustered in Jaffa and Tel Aviv
had been driven into the countryside, where they overwhelmed
the already strapped network of thirty farm villages that stretched

from Metula on the border of Lebanon in the north to Rishon-le-Zion near Gaza in the south.

The town of Zichron Ya'akov, just south of Haifa, had been one of the more prosperous of these Jewish settlements. Founded in the late 1880s, it now boasted sturdy stone houses of European design that lined the paved streets. From a few dozen pioneer families at its start, Zichron Ya'akov's population had swelled to more than a thousand Jewish residents as well as several hundred Arab workmen and their families who lived on the outskirts. It boasted a two-story synagogue plus a large communal barn normally filled with the combined harvests of the community, and a modern hotel that attracted wealthy travelers who paused there during the journey between Haifa and Jerusalem in the south.

But that prosperity had vanished once the war in Europe had begun and, now, an added terror gripped the townspeople. After months of rumor and suspicion it was clear that one of their own leading families was sending detailed reports about the Turkish Army to the British forces poised on the east bank of the Suez Canal. Turkish intelligence had recently found evidence of the spy ring in the area, and if they discovered the Zichron Ya'akov plotters there would be no wasted effort sorting out the innocent from the guilty; the entire community might be exterminated.

Despite their anxiety, the villagers struggled to go on with their rituals of the season and their religion. This was the start of the Hebrew lunar calendar month of *Tishri* that marked four of the most holy periods for the observant. First came the two days of the New Year observance, *Rosh Hashanah*. The next ten days were the Days of Repentance, a period of acknowledging wrongs committed in the previous year. At the end of that came *Yom Kippur*, a Day of Atonement spent fasting and praying in the synagogue.

Then, on October 1, came the ten days of *Sukkot,* a time when families gathered to remember the forty-year journey when Moses led his people out of slavery in Egypt as recounted in *Exodus.* Often referred to as the Feast of Booths, the observance required each family gathering to construct a temporary hut covered with leafy vegetation or palm fronds. There meals would be eaten and prayers of praise and remembrance would be offered. Normally it would be a time of joy. The harvest should have been gathered by then, and in between the times of prayer there would be dancing and song, and the young people of the village could relax and cast appraising glances at likely marriage prospects.

Syria–Palestine had endured more than war. In 1915 a Biblical plague of locusts devoured almost every living plant and proved fatal to livestock. In that year and in the two that followed, the twenty thousand–man force that was the Ottoman Fourth Army of Turks and Germans now occupying the province had routinely pillaged the Jewish farms of scant reserves of grain and seized nearly all the livestock to support their successive campaigns to capture the Suez Canal and drive the British from Egypt.

In a bitter irony, when the Ottoman offensives of 1915 and 1916 ended in defeat, Turkish officials fixed the blame on the Jews themselves. Beginning in the summer of 1917 Jewish residents of Jaffa and Tel Aviv were expelled into the countryside. The people of Zichron Ya'akov, already pressed to the limits of endurance, were terrified that the Turkish suspicions of Jewish subversion would be justified if the spies among them were discovered.

The Aaronsohn family was to blame, even their friends were forced to admit that. It had become apparent to everyone in the community that something dangerous had been going on for more than a year. Strangers had been seen at the sprawling compound of the family's patriarch, Ephraim Aaronsohn, on Founders

Street. And at the agricultural experiment station founded by the eldest son Aaron ten miles away at the tiny coastal hamlet of Athlit, there were rumors that a British ship could be spotted at anchor offshore at night. Most of the gossip focused on Sarah, the older of Ephraim's daughters, whose behavior in recent months had been suspicious—indeed some said scandalous. She clearly was up to no good.

In truth, the Aaronsohns had never been popular in Zichron Ya'akov. They had been prominent and influential, but their prosperity and prominence caused offended feelings among some of the other early settlers. This was despite the fact that Ephraim had been one of the first pioneer families to arrive in Palestine in the 1880s. And Aaron had become an international celebrity for his discoveries on improving the impoverished soil of the region. As a teenager he had become a protégé of the powerful French Baron Edmond de Rothschild and had been a conduit of much of the charitable subsidies that flowed into the village from the baron and from wealthy Jews in the United States. That influence and Aaron's habit of allocating most of the funds only to those who backed his schemes added resentment to the envy that had long simmered below the surface among many villagers.

But now Aaron, as well as three other siblings, had vanished. Some said they were in America living in luxury. Others said they were in Cairo with the British plotting an insurrection against the Turks that would get everyone killed. This had left Sarah in charge of both the family home and the strange goings-on at Athlit. Earlier in September the village elders had become so alarmed at the suspicious activity that a delegation had warned her to either cease spying or face reprisals—even denunciation to the Turks. She had not denied the accusations but merely had asked for time to respond.

Now it seemed it was too late for the spies to disband and be rescued by the British. Patrols of watchmen along the beach had been doubled. Mounted Ottoman gendarmerie had been searching the passes through the hills to the south and the desert vastness beyond. The Kaimakan, the chief magistrate of Haifa, had been going from village to village demanding information about treason among the Jews.

But Zichron Ya'akov clung to its customs. On the first day of *Sukkot* one of the prominent families invited everyone to an afternoon celebration of their son's marriage betrothal. Sarah went to the festivities, to represent the Aaronsohn family and to show her neighbors that she was unafraid of the threats. While the party was not nearly as lavish as it might have been in more prosperous times, everyone put on a cheerful face once the music and dancing began.

Some of the celebrants noticed that Sarah suddenly was called outside by one of the Arab workers from the Athlit station. Turkish police had been to his nearby village looking for spies and specifically asked about her by name. Without taking leave of her hosts, she quickly saddled her horse and hurried to Athlit. She spent the rest of the day burning incriminating documents, including the final intelligence reports she had hoped to send to Cairo when the British ship made its next visit. She also dismissed all the experiment station's Arab workers, telling them to return to their villages and, if questioned, deny all knowledge of the spy ring's activities.

As evening approached, she made her way back to her father's home, which was a compound of three buildings that fronted on the main thoroughfare, Founders Street. She felt a twinge of guilt for not having prepared the ritual *Sukkot* meal for the start of this important holy period. But the house was dark and empty. There was no sign of her father Ephraim or brother

Zvi. Before she could speculate why they had not begun to build the small hut out of palm fronds for the observance, there was a pounding on the door and shouts for her to open it.

There in the gathering darkness stood a Turkish sergeant of the gendarmerie and several others in uniforms. The sergeant demanded to know if she was the daughter of Ephraim Aaronsohn and when she said she was, they grabbed her roughly by the arms and half-dragged her out of the house toward the street. Her protests and demands to know what was going on were met with stolid silence.

On most days Founders Street was busy with local farmers and merchants and with travelers pausing on journeys between Haifa and Jerusalem to stay at the town's hotel. Evenings normally also saw neighbors strolling up and down, pausing at gates to visit with each other. But not now. The afternoon party had quickly broken up at the approach of the Turkish police. All the houses were now shuttered, not a glimmer of lamplight could be seen within. Zichron Ya'akov was holding its breath in fear of attracting a glance from the Turks.

At the far end of Founders Street stood a large house that had been commandeered as a jail and interrogation center for suspects. That night Sarah found Turkish soldiers crowding into the front room, where a long table had been set in a circle of lighted lamps.

Sarah recognized the two officers at the table: one was the Kaimakan, the chief magistrate from Haifa. The other was the *gendarmerie sefi,* the head of the militarized police force for the area. Both were sitting stiffly, trying to maintain the dignity of their offices while conveying deadly menace to her. After a glance at some papers on the desk, the magistrate asked her sharply, "Are you the Jewess Abraham?"

Sarah replied calmly that Abraham was the name of her husband in Constantinople but that since she had returned home to her family she was known here in Zichron Ya'akov as Sarah Aaronsohn. This drew a sly smirk from the policeman as if he had trapped her in an admission. "Then I bring greetings to you from Colonel Bek who says to tell Sarah Aaronsohn that he had long suspected her and her family of being traitors to the government and spies for the enemy British."

This was an unwelcome disclosure. Colonel Aziz Bek was the head of the counterintelligence service of the Turkish Fourth Army that was challenging the British on the battle lines that fronted the Suez Canal. Bek had been chief of police in Constantinople when Sarah had lived there. He was dreaded for having a razor-sharp mind and an animalistic cruelty in dealing with suspects.

Sarah judged that if Colonel Bek had already singled out the Aaronsohn family, then the two local officials confronting her in the makeshift interrogation center were on no mere fishing expedition. The time left to the spy operation known as NILI that she had directed over these few perilous months would now be numbered in hours, not days.

Before she could respond, the police chief nodded to the soldiers who had arrested her. She was half-carried to the rear to an empty room. As she was hurried past other rooms she could only glimpse the huddled forms of men lying in the dim light of the enclosures. One face leaped out at her as she was rushed by: it appeared to be one of her brothers, Zvi, but she must be mistaken. His face was so bruised and distorted; his staring eyes did not show that he recognized her.

Her horror grew when two soldiers appeared from another room with her father between them. Ephraim was dazed and helpless. She was abruptly returned to the front room where she protested to the two Turkish officials, but they paid no attention. Ephraim was held limply upright by his two captors as the Kaimakan began to shout at him that he knew all about the secret spy organization the old man was directing on behalf of the British enemy. He knew that the spy group called itself the NILI, whatever that might mean. Who were their agents? the policeman demanded. What information about the Ottoman armies in Palestine had the NILI given the British? What plans did the British have to invade Palestine, and when?

Sarah's fears mingled with surprise. It was clear that the Turks knew very little about the NILI spies, and they were certainly wrong to suspect her father of being the mastermind. Ephraim had known about the NILI ring that his eldest son Aaron had founded in 1915 and that Sarah, his most loved elder daughter, was now directing. Although her father was in his sixties, thirty-five years of grinding labor in the fields of Zichron Ya'akov had taken its toll; the death of his beloved wife Malkah two years earlier had left him sad and withdrawn. While he had been deliberately kept from knowing the details of the NILI operations, he was aware of the peril to his family and stubborn enough to keep silent.

Summoning some of his old dignity, Ephraim tried to deal with the judge by assuring him that he had always had correct dealings with the Ottoman officials in Haifa, that there had to be some terrible mistake. His oldest son, Aaron, was away pursuing his scientific studies; another son, Alexander, now lived in Cyprus. He did not know where other people were that were named to him. He had never heard the word NILI before. There were no British spies in Zichron Ya'akov.

When the judge coldly called him a liar, Ephraim managed a weak smile and a shrug; he could say no more than what he had said. Sarah felt a brief surge of pride at her father's bravery, but she was very much afraid at what would happen next. Djamal Pasha, the Ottoman's ruling authority over all Syria–Palestine, had come in 1915 fresh from directing the start of the genocide of Turkey's Armenian population. More recently he had ordered the execution of hundreds of Arab leaders who were merely suspected of sympathizing with the revolt against Turkish rule that had begun among the Arab desert tribes to the south. Torture had preceded nearly all of those executions. With Colonel Aziz Bek as his enforcer, other Ottoman officials had learned at their own peril to be merciless.

At his nod the Turkish soldiers moved with practiced ease. Ephraim was forced to kneel on a chair and securely tied in place. While the sergeant forcibly held her father's head erect so he was forced to stare into the eyes of his inquisitors, the two soldiers began to beat the soles of his bare feet with supple canes. They measured each stroke to alternate the pain and they continued even after the swelling had burst blood vessels on his soles and sent Ephraim into a cycle of screaming and fainting that would be revived by each new stroke. Known as *bastinado*, the Turks by legend used this form of torture as a first stage in interrogation because while the pain was unendurable it kept subjects alive for more intense interrogation later.

To her horror, Sarah was forced to watch while her broken father had ceased to cry for mercy and had lapsed into mumbling prayers for deliverance in the Romanian Yiddish he had foresworn forty years earlier when, like most new settlers, he had pledged to speak only in the pure Hebrew of the new Israel.

Finally, the magistrate and police chief rose from their chairs as Ephraim was dragged past Sarah and dropped into one of the rooms to the rear. The magistrate announced that the two officials would go to the hotel for needed refreshment, but when they returned they expected the information they required from the newest Jewish spy who had been brought to them. Coldly he turned to look at Sarah before they left and she knew her turn was next.

She must hold out. She had determined that nothing be revealed. She alone knew all of the inner workings of the NILI organization and the identities of the more than sixty people who provided it with its flow of critical intelligence. Sarah had become the most central figure in the vast NILI network that she and her brothers had created over the last two years. More crucially, she alone also held a great secret. A vast British expeditionary force had been formed in Egypt under General Edmund Henry Hynman Allenby, and it was poised to launch a lightning attack on the Turks with the goal of capturing the regional capital of Jerusalem. Using intelligence Sarah had gathered from the NILI network, notably their secret maps of the Bedouin wells that dotted the arid Gaza desert, Allenby intended to bypass the heavily fortified coastal roads of Palestine and flank the entrenched Ottoman positions.

The British attack could come any day now, any hour. It was imperative that Allenby be warned that the NILI group was in peril. Sarah knew she had to endure the soldiers' tortures and not reveal where the other NILI spies could be found. But equally important, she had to find a way to break free of her torturers long enough to contact the British once more. It could bring rescue and liberation for her and her compatriots, but more important, the Ottoman hold on Palestine must be broken if Israel were to become more than a fragile dream.

As one admirer would claim later, Sarah Aaronsohn was about to become the Joan of Arc of Israel.

CHAPTER ONE

Who Was Sarah Aaronsohn?

•••••••••••••••••••••

1890–1905

Sarah Aaronsohn on her horse, Tayar, ca. 1917

In the early spring of 1917, when Sarah Aaronsohn was briefly in Cairo, she was a shadow of her former self. Just three years before, the twenty-four-year-old bride had been the picture of robust, healthy beauty. Sarah was what we would today judge to be of moderate height, but then she was taller than most girls in her village. With a high, proud bosom and small waist, Sarah's firm stride testified to her long girlhood spent as an active horse-woman in the Carmel foothills beyond the town. Her fine fea-tures were dominated by the same piercing direct gaze of other Aaronsohns, and the same coppery golden hair that caused her Arab neighbors to stare at her.

But now the gaiety and laughter that had sprung from her so readily had been lost by the privations of three years of war and the Turkish military's ransacking of Syria–Palestine's crops and livestock. She had lost considerable weight along with her carefree humor. But in their place she had gained the cold deter-mined stare of the zealot who faced death as a necessary risk for the cause for which she fought. The war had certainly changed Sarah. She had been a proud optimistic pioneer in a new land that offered the dream of an *Eretz Israel,* the Biblical *Zion* for the world's dispossessed Jews. Now she had become a hardened warrior to keep that flickering dream alive. However, history ordained a different path for the Aaronsohn family and especially for Sarah.

Sarah's entire life had been one of constant change and meta-morphosis. Had Ephraim and Malkah Aaronsohn remained in Romania, Sarah would have been confined to the traditional role of young Jewish women of that time and place. She would have been an apprentice to her mother, a servant to her father and brothers, and, in time, sent into an arranged marriage where her status may have improved but the cloistered life of the ghetto would have continued its cycle.

From what is known about the parents, and about Sarah herself, it is unlikely she would have lived a passive existence devoid of confrontation. The Aaronsohns were assertive in their beliefs and aggressive in making their way in the hostile world of late–nineteenth-century Eastern Europe. Ephraim had built his fortune first as a farmer and innkeeper. But he used self-taught expertise in agriculture and hydrology to become the steward of several large farms near Bacau that were owned by absentee Romanian landlords. Malkah, something of a beauty in her youth, added prestige to the marriage since she was the daughter of a leading rabbi. Though little interested in scholarly pursuits, Malkah through her forceful personality stressed the building of strong character in her children.

By the 1880s, the always perilous position of Jewish communities in Eastern Europe became unbearably dangerous. The once-great empires of the Hapsburgs, the Romanovs, and the Ottoman Sultanate were in a sclerosis of decline that rekindled dreams of their subject people for independence. Old frictions over religious identity—Roman Catholic versus Orthodox Christian versus Muslim—were inflamed by conflicts over national identity.

Jews suddenly became the target of convenience in the struggle for power. Pogroms, once an episodic threat, suddenly became the increasing resort of paranoid governments and violent mobs alike. While there had been random anti-Jewish attacks long before, the systematic targeting of Jewish communities began after the assassination of Russia's Tsar Alexander II in 1881. The next year, Alexander III blamed Russian Jews for his father's murder and decreed harsh reprisals on the Jewish communities within his empire. Three years of violence erupted and was duplicated throughout much of Eastern Europe.

A wave of migration and flight had begun in the decade before; those Jews who had the means or helpful relatives abroad set out for more welcoming nations in Western Europe or North and South America. At the same time within the Jewish communities of Russia, Poland, and the Balkans the historical dream of a Jewish nation was reignited. Well before the better known

Zionist organizations of their Western European coreligionists took shape, the *Hibbat Zion* ("love of Zion") movement spread from Russia across the Tsar's mandated Jewish zone, the Pale, throughout Ashkenazi communities of Eastern Europe. Ephraim Aaronsohn was an early convert to the movement. His once-prosperous business was now threatened. And he now had two sons, Aaron, six, and Zvi, four. In his search for a better future for his family, the *Hibbat Zion* message was attractive. It renewed the millennium-old cry that only by returning to Palestine and reestablishing a homeland, could Jews be really safe from the endless Diaspora to foreign lands where they never could find a place. And to make Palestine a true *Eretz Israel,* Jews had to reclaim the land, to farm it, and not only grow their own sustenance but secure their own nation and lasting peace.

So in 1882 the four Aaronsohns were among the most prominent of what became known as the *First Aliyah* ("ascension") to migrate to Palestine. While the movement had at its base a deeply religious, almost mystical core, an important and often overlooked element was the financial and political support its adherents received from evangelical Christians as well as Jews in high positions in Western nations, most notably in Britain, France, and the United States. The support of the major industrial economies provided needed financial backing and, perhaps more important, the tacit protection of the great powers as movement leaders like Aaronsohn sought to inject themselves into a land rife with suspicion, corruption, and the threat of violent reaction against them.

Everyone, it seemed, had a reason to want the Jews to return to Palestine. Not least of these were the governments of the European powers who viewed the early flood of these exotic refugees into their own cities as an unwanted addition to their troubles keeping their political power stable. Indeed, some of the Sephardic Jewish community leaders who had gained both prosperity and a measure of acceptance in the major capitals were alarmed at the arrival of these Ashkenazi Jews from the East, with their strange countenances, coarse manners, and dialects. It would be better for all concerned if "those people" could be resettled somewhere else. Syria–Palestine appeared ideal.

Ignored by both the monarchs of Europe and Zionist adherents were the Jews who had remained in Syria–Palestine for centuries after the Roman diaspora. They were called the Yishuv (later, the Old Yishuv), and were deeply Orthodox communities who survived in enclaves in the four holy cities of Judaism: Jerusalem, Hebron, Tiberias, and Safed. Strictly controlled by their rabbis, these scholarly communities were largely dependent on *Halukka*, donations from Jews elsewhere in the world in return for prayers in their behalf. The arrival of a wave of new immigrants with their independent ways was an immediate threat to the Yishuv. The world beyond Palestine suddenly seemed too close for comfort.

Recall that today's world of seemingly constant change got underway in the nineteenth century, when the technological explosions of industrialization challenged centuries of control that monarchies had held over the creation of wealth and the mobility of citizens. A power structure that saw life for most people unchanged since medieval times was vanishing, to be replaced by—what?

This explosion had at its core the harnessing of new sources of energy that had begun a century earlier. Each new fuel exploited—from wood to coal and then to petroleum—released a quantum more power to enhance mankind's ambitions. Regions that possessed an abundance of this energy—North America,

Persia, the Crimea, and, potentially, Arabia—suddenly became targets of exploitation. Ancient empires—the British, French, Russian, and Ottoman—were jolted out of their slumbers and now raced to modernize in order to keep pace with the destabilizing forces that accompanied the new prosperity. The richer they got, the more energy they needed. The more that Western civilizations produced miracles of industry, communications, culture, and learning, the more poverty and injustice threatened the whole global structure. As steamships, railroads, and telegraphs shrank the globe, the lures and perils of modernity awakened distant corners of the world that had slumbered for centuries. This rude awakening was as frightening as it was exciting. Revolution of all kinds was in the air.

The Ottoman Empire was far from immune. When Russia's Tsar Nicholas I called Turkey "the sick man of Europe," he was not referring to some decrepit backwater empire slowly expiring from corruption and neglect—although both diseases festered within the Sublime Porte, the central bureaucracy that served the sultans. Rather, Nicholas presciently observed that the Turks were being caught in the same web as he, having to seek ever-growing volumes of loans from foreign banking houses and rival governments to fund modernization projects, loans that put the borrowers in ever greater bondage to forces beyond their control. It was a tiger that could neither be ridden for long nor dismounted from safely.

Sultan Abdul Aziz (and his nephew and penultimate successor Abdul Hamid II) became widely photographed celebrities in the 1860s on their visits to the major capitals of Europe. Such was his importance as a potential customer for British capital goods, Queen Victoria marked an 1867 official visit by Aziz by investing a slate of new Knights of the Garter that included the

Sultan along with Tsar Alexander II and Emperor Franz Joseph of Austria–Hungary.

This was a tinseled era when crowned heads and lesser princelings could call each other cousins (with some reason in many cases) and smooth out international disputes by personal correspondence or a tactical marriage. Turkey was merely an acute case. Indeed Abdul Hamid II was reported to have French lineage through one of his grandmothers. But aside from an affinity for the West, the Sultanate had more pressing reasons to court the support of the major powers. From the Balkans to farthest Arabia, the subjects of Ottoman rule chafed at the pervasive corruption and calculated cruelty of their masters. Nationalist movements were being plotted in coffeehouses and Bedouin tents across the Empire. Most pressing of all, the Turks were being harried by a series of losing skirmishes with Russia for hegemony over the oil-rich regions on their shared borders.

So Tsar Nicholas's rueful observation was correct. More than even Russia, the sultans embarked on an orgy of foreign borrowing and ambitious projects to yank their empire into modern times. A network of railroads slowly began to link Constantinople north to the capitals of Europe and south toward the farthest shores of the Arabian Gulf. Telegraph lines tracked along the railroads, postal service was regularized, universities were founded, and even cautious attempts at constitutional reform were tried.

By the time Abdul Hamid II took power in 1876 Turkey boasted the third largest navy in the world, lagging behind only Britain and France. A young cadre of military officers were being sent abroad (most to Germany) to learn modern tactics and public administration. Seven years after he seized power in a coup, the famed Orient Express luxury train began service to Paris and brought adventurers from a dozen nations with ambitious schemes for even greater advancement. Like its European role models, the Porte under Hamid now could afford to create a thoroughly modern secret police network and to invent a unified cultural identity for Turkey. Among the consequences was a ruthless suppression of dissent and the start of a systematic expulsion of non-Turkish minority groups that ultimately led at the start of World War I to the genocidal eradication of millions of Armenian subjects. It would not stop there.

One of the more fascinating of the promoters to arrive in Constantinople was the fifty-three-year-old Laurence Oliphant. He was a former Member of Parliament, a London *Times* war correspondent, a popular novelist, and, not least, a former British Foreign Office spy in the Orient and Middle East. Oliphant had in midlife turned into an ardent Zionist. He was one of those exotic personalities generated during the Victorian era. Often sketchily educated, their natural intellect led them to become fascinated in equal amounts with desolate regions, primitive people and strange causes, either religious or political. They could be brilliant or they could be outright loony but somehow straitlaced British society tolerated them.

Oliphant had become a convert of a tiny communal sect based in America on the shores of Lake Erie. Like many American and British evangelical Christians, he believed that Jews must reclaim the Holy Land of Palestine as a prerequisite to the Biblical prophecies of the Second Coming of Jesus Christ. Despite his mysticism, Oliphant also became a skilled fundraiser among likeminded evangelicals in America and especially in the higher ranks of the British government. His cause was also helped by the fact that in the late 1870s the Prime Minister was Benjamin Disraeli, who endorsed Oliphant's plan to buy large tracts of land in Palestine for resettlement of his coreligionists from Eastern Europe.

Nor was Oliphant averse to personal profit. His evangelistic zeal was elastic enough to allow him to represent the interests of prominent British financial and railroad interests in a dead-heat race with German and French promoters to win rail and oil concessions from the Turks. His patron was Edward Cazalet, the leading investor in schemes to link a network of railroads throughout the Balkans to better exploit the rich oil fields of the Caucasus and Persia.

It is unclear just how the forces of Cazalet and Oliphant first made contact with Ephraim Aaronsohn and other well-heeled leaders of the Romanian Jewish community. Oliphant had made one unsuccessful bid in 1879 to win Ottoman permission for his resettlement plans. What is clear is that in 1882 he returned to Constantinople with a few hundred *Aliyah* adherents from Romania and that Ephraim Aaronsohn was among them. Instead of trying to trudge their way through the bewildering corridors of Ottoman bureaucracy, the Oliphant delegation made its first call on General Lew Wallace, the American ambassador, himself a pro-Zionist.

Wallace had been a Civil War general and the governor of the New Mexico territory where he had set in motion events that led to the shooting of legendary killer William Bonney, a.k.a. Billy the Kid. He also had been the author of the wildly popular novel about the heroic Jewish slave-charioteer, *Ben Hur: A Tale of the Christ*. Arriving in Constantinople in 1881, Wallace quickly became one of the most trusted of the foreign advisers of Abdul Hamid II in his efforts to modernize his Empire.

This time the Oliphant delegation, with Wallace's support, quickly won the Sultan's permission to buy land for Jewish settlement south of Haifa near the end of the Mount Carmel mountain range. Using the funds he had raised in London, Oliphant and his wife moved to Palestine with the settlers but divided their time between the European quarter of Haifa and a village of Druze in the shadow of the Mount itself. The *First Aliyah*—literally, "the Act of Returning"—back to the Biblical homeland of *Eretz Israel* of the Jews scattered centuries earlier by the Diaspora was now underway in earnest.

The land for the sixty-five *aliyot* families was located ten miles farther along at the edge of the range, near the coastal road that linked Haifa with Hadera and Jerusalem farther south. It was a woebegone hamlet named Zamarin that could barely sustain a handful of Arab peasants. It was a dismal place, dominated on one side by the Carmel hills and on the seaward side by the tall ruins of a Crusaders' castle.

Disaster loomed from the start. Those settlers with actual farming experience had dealt with fertile land that had been cleared and prepared centuries before. The land the Ottomans had allocated was a near-barren mix of malarial swamp and arid hard-packed soil pocked with boulders. The task of draining the swamps and channeling the water onto the dry land was back-breaking work made all the harder as malaria decimated their ranks. By the end of the first year, nearly half the settlers had died or fled back to Europe, seeking sanctuary with relatives in the crowded Jewish ghettos of major cities.

But Ephraim Aaronsohn was made of sterner stuff. Like a few others, he had come with financial resources that enabled him to endure the early years. The settlers who survived the first years also broke with two of the assumptions of the *Aliyah* movement's early founders. While many of the projects and ventures they undertook were communal in structure— road-building, irrigation canals, and storage barns—neverthe-less, each family plotted out their own land for their private profit. Secondly, the Aaronsohns ignored the notion that only the Jews themselves should work their land. They bypassed the de facto segregation that kept older settlements of Arab peasants, Yishuv Jews, and Palestinian Christians separate. Ephraim was an early employer of Arab workers, paying good wages and establishing respectful albeit cautious relations with the elders of the nearby villages.

In this outreach to their Arab neighbors, Ephraim was echoing the dream of the theoretical founder of the Zionist movement, Theodore Hetzl, who argued for an *Eretz Israel* for Jews where religious practice would be a strictly personal matter. More, Herzl believed that Jews who migrated to Palestine would be welcomed by the Arab peasantry once they saw they would share in the benefits of the husbandry and new technologies that the European *aliyots* would bring with them.

Life in the early years was not all drudgery for Malkah and Ephraim. Children, and lots of them, were crucial not only for assuring a family's future, but also to preserve the fabric of the larger community. Ephraim and Malkah had arrived in Palestine with two young sons, Aaron, who was six, and Zvi, age four. After their arrival the couple's first daughter was born, but soon died. In the next decade two more sons, Shmuel and Alexander, would be born, while two other daughters would die in infancy. In 1890, Sarah was born, followed two years later by the couple's sixth child to survive, Rivka.

By the time Sarah was born, the identity of the Aaronsohn family was firmly established as an amalgam of the personas of Ephraim and Malkah and the realities of their new home in Palestine. Like Ephraim and her brothers, Sarah was strong and energetic. From Malkah, Sarah and her brothers inherited a fierce dignity that stemmed from the mother's heritage as the daughter of a distinguished rabbi back in Romania and her family's claim to be directly descended from King David. The Aaronsohns had forceful direct personalities that could be abrasive.

They were a self-contained society and stood out with the broader Jewish communal culture of their neighbors. That broader culture had been forged by many forces, the persecution of the people and governments in the lands where the Diaspora had taken them, the dependency of Jews on each other for survival, and, not least, the strict adherence to the rituals of their Biblical faith that sustained their souls. The Aaronsohns, while observant, were not religious, nor were they especially communal in their ties to their neighbors. They stood apart, and while the other pioneers at work in Zichron Ya'akov respected Ephraim and his sons for their diligence, there was an envious suspicion that the family thought themselves better than others. To an extent the envy was well founded.

Much had changed in the eight years since the first *aliyots* had arrived in Palestine. The nameless communes of crude shelters had become a network of prosperous villages funded by a wealthy benefactor whose tightly managed funds transformed the farmers from survivalists into developers of a diverse mix of exportable foods and products. The village the Aaronsohns called home was one of the earliest of these new creations and it had a new name—Zichron Ya'akov—that honored the father of their new wealthy patron, French Baron Edmond de Rothschild.

Faced with the prospect of famine and failure, the leaders of the *aliyot* pioneers had almost immediately begun to importune wealthy Jews in Europe to come to their aid. By the end of 1882 they had attracted the interest of Baron de Rothschild, who, while an heir to the wide banking network of his famous family, was not interested in (or perhaps not encouraged to participate in) its highly complex enterprises.

For much of his life Baron Edmond had devoted his time to building up his soon-to-be-legendary wine chateaus, as well as amassing a huge collection of art and founding a number of scientific research institutes in France and elsewhere in Europe. As a sponsor of several French archaeological expeditions into Syria–Palestine, he became interested in the prospects of the region and so, when the *aliyots* approached him, he was primed to respond. He abandoned his art collecting and began assembling technical managers—most from vineyard plantations in French North African colonies—to oversee the building of modern housing, schools and roads, and the development of crops—grapes, dates, citrus, honey—that could be sold in the market at Haifa and profitably exported abroad.

The baron had complex motivations. He had become a convinced Zionist. The project, if managed properly, would also prove his worth to his financier brothers and cousins. And then there was his wine. For twenty years France's famed wineries had seen vineyards destroyed by a *phylloxera* aphid that attacked the roots of the vines. So new pest-free vineyards would be planted in Palestine, and the wine not dedicated for sacramental purposes would be barreled and exported to Europe's thirsty markets. In addition to the vineyards, one of his first projects was to build two state-of-the-art wineries, the first at Zichron Ya'akov. Ephraim Aaronsohn became one of its director-managers.

It takes an effort to imagine the transformation the early *aliyots* underwent in the first decade of their time in Palestine. Only a few years before they had escaped the state-sanctioned terrorism of the pogroms. The land they came to first appeared almost uninhabitable. They were viewed askance by the Yishuv communities and warily by their Arab neighbors. Disease and disenchantment decimated their ranks.

And now, thanks to Baron Rothschild's infusion of an estimated $50 million (in nineteenth-century dollars), modern villages with good schools, synagogues, roads, and solidly built stone houses were rising up around them. Now they could keep the observances of their faith without fear even as they built a future for their children. Now there was no ghetto to confine them and they knew the heady freedom of living in their own land.

It was in this new village of Zichron Ya'akov that Sarah came of age and blossomed. From childhood, she had early taken on the intense and outgoing personalities of two of her brothers, Aaron and Alexander. The two other brothers, Zvi and Shmuel, and the baby sister Rivka, born in 1892, tended to be more passive and content. But not Sarah. She was taller than most girls of the village and well aware of her robust, athletic figure. She had an easy laugh and loved to dance. But her eyes mirrored the intensity and impatience of Aaron and Alexander.

In many respects, Sarah's evolution from what she might have been had the family stayed in Romania to what she was becoming mirrored the development of Zichron Ya'akov. They both kept a firm footing in the traditions of Judaism and the family but both expanded and flowered as the land around them was tamed and restored to its Biblical paradise. Both were open, modern, and expansive.

She remained a dutiful and affectionate daughter all her life even as she advanced into modern times. She became the best seamstress in the village and fashioned dresses for herself and others that were skillful copies of the fashions that appeared in the latest European magazines. But there was a wild curiosity that drove Sarah. At twelve she overcame her father's first refusal for a horse of her own. Mounted on Tayar, she prowled the hills and caves in the Carmel range that was the boundary between the coastal villages and the stark Gaza desert beyond the hills. She became a skilled horsewoman and a crack pistol shot, and that reputation along with her remarkable fiery hair earned a wary respect among the more remote Arab villagers who might have interfered with her. She also showed an early talent for easily absorbing languages, at first the often confusing dialects of Arabic that marked the different sects of local Arabs and those of the Bedouin tribesmen who lurked on the Gaza desert wastes on the other side of the Carmel mountain range. It was a talent that she shared with her older brothers Aaron and Alexander.

That same wanderlust drove Sarah to learn apace with her eldest brother Aaron's rapidly expanding library, which emphasized his studies in geology and botany, but also included texts on philosophy and politics. Education of girls in the schools sponsored by Baron de Rothschild came to an end at age twelve and that was certainly enough for Rivka. But Sarah pushed on, becoming an avid reader of Aaron's books in French and German, while becoming fluent in Hebrew and Turkish.

By the time she was fifteen she had become Aaron's secretary and surrogate representative in local farming matters when he was away from Zichron Ya'akov. Aaron was on the move by then and on the verge of becoming an international celebrity. Sarah too was poised for the first steps on the march in her dramatic transformation from what she was to what she has become today.

CHAPTER TWO

Friends in America

• •

1905–1910

Aaron Aaronsohn (1876–1919)

S arah's eldest brother, Aaron Aaronsohn, was a force of nature. Tall, broad-shouldered, and muscular, Aaron had taken his father's entrepreneurial ambition and discipline to another level even as a boy. He had been six years old when the family moved to Palestine. Early on he had been forced into the backbreaking work of older men as they dug the unyielding soil of their new land in a battle simply to survive.

But more than the imposing figure of a man that he became, many observers—including the teachers Baron de Rothschild hired for his village schools—were awed by the fierce intellectual curiosity that pushed Aaron to constantly search the land of Palestine and its flora for ways to improve it, to return it to the proverbial land of milk and honey that Hebrew texts had described. He could be peremptory and brusque with those who did not think as quickly as he, but even those he annoyed recognized his zeal.

Aaron had achieved astonishing progress as a self-taught prodigy in botany, geology, and hydrology—as well as becoming a fluent writer in French and German. The baron concluded from school reports that the lad needed more advanced studies back in Europe, where studies of Middle Eastern agriculture were a hot topic of research at many important universities. So while he was barely in his twenties, Aaron was brought to France from Palestine and sponsored by the baron at a leading agricultural college in Grignon. There Aaron quickly perfected both his French and German pronunciations and began corresponding with crop scientists at the leading institutes in Germany. All these senior academics warmed to the young man's intelligence and fervor and were free with their mentoring.

One motive for such generosity was simple: a need for bread. Millions in Europe and the United States had abandoned farm life for big cities and industrial jobs that were scarcely less rigorous. But now someone must feed them, and the world's wheat crops had hit a plateau of productivity. Traditional breadbasket lands were over-farmed and the varieties of wheat had atrophied somewhat. New techniques were needed and scientists began to study the "dry farming" traditions of Near Eastern crops where heat was intense and water scarce. The search also was on for a genetically untainted wheat—an "Ur-wheat"—that might revive the genetic productivity of crops.

Aaron sent a steady stream of books and letters back to Zichron Ya'akov chronicling his progress and his realization that there could be just such a historic wheat in Palestine—and that he was the one who could find it. To do that, however, he first had to repay his sponsor by returning to Palestine as a kind of project manager as the baron's network of model villages was spreading.

For Sarah, Aaron, and the rest of the Aaronsohns this was a golden time. Of all the baron's villages, Zichron Ya'akov was the most successful. While no one was rich, the remaining settlers were at last free of the fear of starvation, crops were abundant, and the village itself began to attract new arrivals. They had their own doctor living there, a two-story synagogue, and a new European-style hotel proved a popular stop for travelers on the coastal road. The Aaronsohns were prosperous enough to own their own carriage (and employ an Arab driver) for their frequent trips to Haifa twenty miles to the north for vineyard business or pleasure.

When Aaron was home he and his friends would race their horses and meet up with young friends who competed with them in various contests, including excursions into the desert where they kept an eye on the Bedouin who prowled about for stray livestock to pilfer.

Sarah too enjoyed the new freedom. At village dances her gay laughter and love of dancing drew attentive suitors from nearby villages as well as the boys she had grown up with in Zichron. She was popular with other girls as well, all the more so when she got one of the first sewing machines. Like all her friends, Sarah avidly read the popular magazines available from Europe. The new publishing technique of halftone photographs featured celebrities wearing the latest Paris fashions, and Sarah became adept at copying the latest trends in couture for herself and others.

But while she was as adept at the innocent flirting as any young person, no one could penetrate that reserve that kept all Aaronsohns aloof from others. The Aaronsohns' sense of separation would have troubling—if unintended—consequences. As a roving consultant throughout the region where Rothschild villages were being established, Aaron could not help but clash with the French technicians and managers who worked directly for the baron.

For the French, who were used to having dictatorial powers during their colonial careers, this young upstart Jew became an annoyance and then a threat to their control over the development of the villages and their agriculture. Also, not a few of the managers were used to siphoning off funds through kickbacks from local suppliers. Perhaps just as important, Aaron never appreciated that the supervisors themselves were operating under micromanaged orders from the baron himself. Rothschild understandably reasoned that since it was his money, he should have final say.

When Aaron failed to convince village overseers to do as he demanded, he angered them further by writing peremptory letters directly to Rothschild. When charges of incompetence failed to move the baron, Aaron alleged corruption and conflicts of interest. While there is evidence that some of his accusations may have been well founded, the baron found Aaron's tone insulting and, finally, after sending him a letter of rebuke for his insolence and ingratitude, Aaron resigned his post and returned to Zichron Ya'akov free to devote all his time to the search for the "mother of all wheat."

When he returned to Zichron Ya'akov in early 1905, Aaron immediately set out on his search. He prowled the hills and valleys in the Carmel range as far as the desert borders, examining cultivated fields and wild flora in canyon crevasses. At night he found

shelter in the caves that had been refuges since Biblical times.
Sarah, now fifteen and a skilled horsewoman, often followed him
bringing water and supplies, tracking him and fending off threats
from Arab youths and Bedouin livestock poachers.

PREHISTORIC WHEAT FOUND IN PALESTINE

Sought in Vain for Centuries, It Is at Last Encountered in Original Wild Form.

GROWS ON STERILE LANDS

By Cross-Breeding Its Young Discoverer Hopes to Produce a Hardier and Better Type of Wheat.

New York Times, *October 26, 1906*

\Then in the spring of 1906 he spotted in an orchard in
the Galilee a single stalk of what he identified as genetically historic wild wheat. Spurred by that fragile discovery he pushed on
to Mount Herman, where a survey of its western slope proved
fruitless. As an afterthought, Aaron tried the eastern slope of the
mountain and came upon an entire field of the wild wheat.

Aaron's reports and samples were quickly sent to his mentors in Berlin and caused a sensation. His discovery ignited both
controversy and celebrity for a number of reasons. He had raised
the prospect of genetically combining the hardier "Ur-wheat"
(the press quickly dubbed it "the mother of all wheat") with the
more traditional species to create a new productive source of sustenance. At the same time, Aaron's discovery had played into the
heated argument among anthropologists about where the "cradle
of civilization" had its origins.

One of the first to reach out to Aaron was David Fairchild, chief scientist of the U.S. Department of Agriculture in Washington. Fairchild was a recognized expert on Near Eastern agriculture and was part of the "dry farming" movement that sought to expand American wheat-growing regions to some of the arid regions of the western states. To his amazement, Aaron's replies also included a surprising interest and knowledge of the geology, climate, and agronomy of California, which he asserted shared a similar climate and potential with Palestine.

Aaron delayed accepting Fairchild's invitation to come to America at once. A financial crisis had gripped the still-vulnerable Jewish settlements of the region. The flow of project funds from Baron de Rothschild had diminished as more villages began to prove themselves self-sustaining, and now many of the settlers proved unwilling to submit to his management discipline.

The baron and the Aaronsohns both had reasons to be unhappy the way things were turning out in Palestine. Early in the 1900s a *Second Aliyah* was well underway. More than two and a half million Eastern European Jews were fleeing for their lives wherever they could find a haven. Those who could went to South America, Australia, and Canada, but more than half—usually those with relatives already there—headed for the United States.

While only about twenty thousand of these refugees chose to go to Palestine, it was a large enough infusion to exacerbate the friction among these newcomers, the old Yishuv long-time residents, and the *First Aliyah* settlers. As the new century progressed, returning Jews had increased in number to an estimated 43,000. An Ottoman census at the time also counted 57,000 Christian Arabs and a dominant 430,000 Muslim Arabs throughout Syria–Palestine, so the *aliyots* were still a fragile minority.

It was not a unified minority, however. The old Yishuv communities of scholars in the cities had never warmed to the first wave of immigrants. The second wave of newcomers was even more jarring and abrasive to both the rabbinical scholar and early pioneer communities.

These new arrivals were obvious competitors for the support of other European Jewish philanthropists. They also brought a new and disturbing political philosophy with them. The deteriorating politics among the great powers was a driving force behind this *Second Aliyah* movement. The new immigrants headed toward Palestine came from cities in Austria, Germany, and France, as well as the Balkans. These city dwellers, often young men without families, had been converted to variations of Marxist–Socialist doctrines. Backed by ample funds from home, some were merely content to find a new urban environment where they could argue in cafes over philosophy and nurse revolutionary daydreams.

However, many dreamed of reclaiming the land of *Eretz Israel* and farming it. These were the early *kibbutzim* who wanted a communal approach to farming and society, one that stressed total Jewish self-reliance and scorned using neighboring Arab laborers. More problematic for the older immigrants, these new Western Jews openly declared that the Arabs must give way to the historic owners of Israel, that they must live segregated and second-class lives in their homeland even if it took the force of Jewish arms to make it so.

In the United States, philanthropic Jews had been slower than Europeans to come to the Zionist cause. Jews had been part of American life from the earliest colonial times and had played a significant role in helping to finance the Revolutionary War. Later immigrant waves from Austria and Germany in the 1840s had created dynasties in banking and trade that had enabled many families to move into the ranks of the upper middle class.

By 1906 President Theodore Roosevelt appointed Oscar Straus, of the Macy's retailing fortune, to the post as Secretary of Commerce. He later served President William Howard Taft as U.S. Ambassador to the Sultanate in Constantinople; it was the only major diplomatic post abroad that would accept a Jew.

Increasingly frustrated by the diversion away from his scientific studies required by writing begging letters to traditional patrons, Aaron finally decided to accept Fairchild's invitation to visit America in early 1909. He would go to expand his contacts and knowledge within agriculture circles. But also he was intent on meeting influential American Jews who could be recruited to support his dream of building an agriculture experiment station in Palestine.

In a tantalizing coincidence, Aaron was on his trip to America when a visitor arrived in Zichron Ya'akov in July to poke around the ruins of the Crusader castle looming over the beaches at a tiny nearby hamlet known as Athlit. The castle had been the southernmost and one of the most formidable fortifications built by the Crusader knights. In 1903 Baron de Rothschild had bought the lands surrounding it and forced out the Arab fishermen who had built shelters in its ruins. But the farming commune he hoped to install there did not thrive because the soil had been so despoiled over the centuries. Still, the remains of what had been known as the Chateau of the Pilgrims was of intense interest to the young visitor, an Oxford scholar named Thomas Edward Lawrence.

He could not have escaped notice from anyone in Zichron Ya'akov who saw him. Barely five-feet-four-inches tall and with an odd physique of an elongated head, short torso, and dangling arms, the twenty-year-old Thomas Edward Lawrence arrived in the village wearing a shabby jacket, shoes more suited to city streets, and carrying only a small satchel for his personal possessions and notebooks. He would spend that summer on an arduous walking tour that took him a thousand miles from Athlit and Nazareth in the south all the way north to Antioch and the Hittite ruins at Carchemish along the Euphrates River in Mesopotamia. Even at the young age of twenty, Lawrence was busy fashioning a new persona, that of the antiquarian archaeologist-adventurer. Later in life, many of the witnesses to his more fabled role as the heroic Lawrence of Arabia would call him a "fraud" and "imposter" but that is not exactly true. More probably, Lawrence was one of those who so despised how he saw himself that he tried on various personalities to fit the moment, and when the moment passed he could put on another as easily as one changes a costume.

From his earliest memories, young Ned, as his family called him, was surrounded by uncomfortable fictions. Even his last name was a fabrication. His father was an Anglo-Irish landowner named Sir Thomas Chapman who came under the spell of his children's Scottish governess. In Ireland divorce was both a legal and social virtual impossibility, so Chapman abandoned his wife and daughters, gave up his estates, and, taking only a modest settlement, he and his new love left and after casting about first in Wales finally settled down in Oxford in a common-law marriage and middle-class anonymity as the Lawrences.

Sarah, the common-law wife, was something of a tyrant over her husband and her five sons. But Ned, the second oldest, waged a constant revolt and refused to be cowed by the frequent thrashings she administered. Luckily he was able to enroll in a local school that served as a feeder for the fabled university, and there he discovered that the era's popular fascination for stories of the Crusades led him on bicycle excursions to nearby churches where he did brass rubbings of the tombs of famous knights.

Oxford at the time was undergoing a building boom in the center part of the old city and Lawrence and a friend haunted construction sites unearthing artifacts from its ancient history and taking them to the university's famed Ashmolean Museum, which housed a trove of antiquities and a faculty of world-class scholars. His teachers recommended him to a place at Oxford's Jesus College where in 1907 he began to study history and prowled the collections at the Ashmolean. There he came under the eye of its new director, D.G. Hogarth.

Hogarth, then forty-six, was a character out of an adventure novel. A recognized expert on Middle Eastern history, a skilled archaeologist, and able administrator, Hogarth was also a talent-spotter for friends in the British government's higher bureaucracies of the War Department and Foreign Office. At his encouragement, Lawrence undertook summertime bicycle tours of France to study the Crusader castles there as part of a thesis project. From that point on it was inevitable that the young man would go to Syria–Palestine in 1909.

By then, an important feature of the Lawrence persona was fixed, that of the romantic ascetic. Hardened by his mother's angry discipline, the boy had gone further to toughen and test himself. He would go without food and set out ever-longer trips on foot and by bicycle until he was near exhaustion. By the time he reached Zichron Ya'akov on that three-month trek in 1909, he was used to walking astonishing distances and subsisting on the meager hospitality of the Arab and Jewish villages along the way. He certainly took notice of the Aaronsohn home with its pink stone walls and tended gardens but, would he, as some legends have it, have taken equal notice of the then eighteen-year-old Sarah Aaronsohn? More likely, Lawrence was too totally absorbed in his quest for insights into Crusader architecture. He had been warned even by Hogarth that the journey was too arduous and dangerous for an Englishman on his own. Lawrence was determined to return in triumph so he pushed on to Nazareth and then turned northward.

Meanwhile Aaron's own journey was turning into just such a triumph. In a stream of letters to Sarah, he recounted how he and Fairchild had bonded almost at once. Fairchild would later write about his astonishment when Aaron, who arrived speaking no English, quickly learned to speak and write in that language in a matter of weeks. Aaron, in turn, was surprised when Fairchild revealed he had secured an invitation for Aaron to visit his dream state, California, and better still, to go to the premier U.S. agricultural science establishment at the University of California at Berkeley. He found that the region reminded him so much of the climate and potential agricultural diversity of Palestine, that he began to draw immediate parallels. The boom that was going on in California offered the same future for *Eretz Israel*—if only it had the help it needed to flourish.

As an added fillip to his pleasure, Aaron was surprised to learn he had been brought to the university as a prospective candidate to succeed the dean of the agriculture school, and he was offered the post. With some reluctance, he turned down the offer. On his return across the country he visited wealthy Jews in Chicago and other large cities and gave talks urging them to support his plans to accomplish in Palestine what was happening in California. Once he reached New York he secured patronage from figures such as Louis Brandeis, the first Jewish Justice on the U.S. Supreme Court; his protégé attorney Felix Frankfurter; and from financiers such as Straus, Jacob Schiff, Paul Warburg (a relative of Aaron's German scientist mentor Otto Warburg), and, fatefully, Henry Morgenthau. The latter was an early backer of the political ambitions of a dynamic Princeton University president named Woodrow Wilson. In 1913 Morgenthau would succeed Straus as the next U.S. Ambassador to Constantinople.

Sarah, like Aaron, had been on the move as well. In 1907 and 1908, she had gone on a chaperoned tour of Paris, Geneva, Berlin, and Rome perfecting her French and German, broadening her experience of the modern world, and learning the latest sewing techniques. Her fluency in French and German rounded out the language skills she would need back in Zichron, in addition to Hebrew, Yiddish, and the Arab dialects of the area. She had become a very polished young woman. She had reveled in the cosmopolitan surroundings of Paris and Rome. Now back in Zichron Ya'akov, she had become familiar enough with the classifications of botany to arrange the collection of specimens arriving from Aaron's travels and to oversee the library he had started. She was rapidly becoming a woman of the new century. Would she have even noticed the travel-stained Englishman who passed by her door any more than the self-absorbed Lawrence would have noticed her?

Aaron's stay in America was a triumph on a number of fronts. In a series of speeches that attracted press coverage and in personal interviews, Aaron convinced even resolute anti-Zionists that an agricultural breakthrough in a revived Palestine could produce enormous benefits of international importance. He returned to Palestine at the end of 1910 with $20,000 in contributions and an American legal charter from the leading U.S. Zionist group to establish an agricultural research station to explore ways to revive the region to its Biblical fruitfulness.

Aaron managed at once to acquire a site for the new research facility in the tiny failed village of Athlit, which perched above the beach on the Mediterranean shore nestled in the shadow of the ruined Crusader castle. The plot was a good location just a few miles from Zichron Ya'akov and adjacent to the coastal road to Haifa. The soil at the site had been terribly despoiled over centuries, but Aaron insisted on buying it so he could prove that his techniques could restore even the most barren land.

While Aaron's international reputation was as a botanist, he also had devoted considerable study to that most precious of agricultural ingredients—water. He had started with old Biblical texts describing the lush gardens and vineyards of the fabled metropolis of Caesarea, which spread along the coast at the base of the same Carmel mountain range. Surely the water that fed those gardens lay buried beneath the arid, sandy wasteland of Athlit, and merely required drilling deep enough to find it. So in addition to the vital infusion of American cash, Aaron's sponsors sent along drilling equipment and a windmill that soon was providing all the irrigation he needed.

Aaron and Sarah spent that winter of 1910–1911 supervising the construction of the greenhouses, a herbarium, and planting beds, as well as organizing a comfortable book-filled library that was moved from Zichron Ya'akov. That year and the next would be remembered by the Aaronsohn family as a hopeful time. Their orchards and vineyards at Zichron were flourishing with harvests that commanded ample cash from the market and exporters of Haifa. Relations with their Arab neighbors—which had always been tentative—seemed to improve as more jobs were made available to the local workers in nearby villages. Aaron was totally immersed in his research and not above taking satisfaction in his international status. Sarah too was happy as she grew in independence in her own right and also in importance as her brother's trusted aide.

But events far away from Palestine were to bring that happy time to an abrupt and frightening end.

CHAPTER THREE

The Three Pashas

•••••••••••••••••••••

1911–1913

Djamal Pasha, Governor of Greater Syria and Palestine

In the decades after their arrival in the 1880s, the earliest *aliyots* could hope that they could find a way of working together with the indigenous Arab *fellaheen* even though they would live apart. After all, there was the shared problem of an Ottoman government, whose officials rarely stirred from their provincial headquarters in Damascus and Haifa unless it was to levy new taxes for their own use or for the absentee wealthy landlords who had influence in Constantinople.

It was an irony of that early time that the Sultan's representatives were so indolent, inefficient, and corrupt that systematic oppression was unlikely. If one could not avoid some levy or demand, a discreet payment to a local official could usually win an exemption. The Empire itself was a huge tapestry of so many restive people from the Balkans all the way to the Arabian Gulf that it had become too huge to control.

In 1880 the Aaronsohns immigrated to Palestine, and the British preempted the vast regions of the Sultan's principality of Egypt. London had to ensure absolute security over their Suez Canal lifeline to India and the rest of their own empire. Other bits of the Ottoman fabric began to fray. It became clear that the lands that had been ruled by the Ottoman Turks since 1299 were caught in the contradictions of its medieval structure and the need to catch up to the modern world.

The truth was that Turkey had always been an artificial creature from the time Osman I had led his warrior tribe from Turkmenistan to subject rival tribes, founded his empire, and lent a variation of his name to the new entity: Ottoman. Osman's successors had grown unimaginably wealthy standing at the gateway through which so much of the known world's commerce passed between China and the merchant states of Europe during the Middle Ages. The constant challenges from their own campaigns of conquest—north through the Balkans to the gates of Vienna or south to the Arabian Sea—created as many problems as triumphs for an empire that could not be efficiently administered territory or fully absorb its sullen, restive subjects.

Worse was the corruption of the Ottoman soul. The once proud, ruthless warriors kept their disdain for the conquered even as they gave way to a grudging toleration for the myriad people within their borders. Rather than make Turks of them all, successive Sultans allowed an arbitrary tolerance that enabled Greeks, Serbians, Armenians, and Jews to prosper as craftsmen, merchants, and even to gain influence as officials within the Sublime Porte itself. Only the Arabs, despite being coreligionists, seemed especially despised, perhaps because the desert princes ruled over the two holy places of Mecca and Medina, prizes the Sultans—who also ruled as head of the Muslim Caliphate—jealously eyed. Meanwhile, successive Sultans became licentious paranoiacs as their seraglios of wives schemed and murdered to advance the futures of their sons and keep their own throats uncut.

Neither Sultan Hamid II nor his advisers contemplated a huge influx of Jews (or any other ethnic group) into the empire. The *aliyots* were viewed as a useful political counterweight in pacifying the restive Arab farmers and herdsmen of the Palestinian region. Ottoman officials in Palestine at first had been grudging but acquiescent to the first wave of Jews who arrived. After all, Jewish merchants and religious leaders had long found a degree of tolerance in Constantinople and other cities that had not existed in Eastern Europe. The Aaronsohns and their group had willingly forsaken the protection of their Romanian passports and become Turkish citizens, albeit of the lower class accorded to all non-Muslims.

That peaceful respite would end as the second decade of the twentieth century began. Independence movements had bubbled everywhere beneath the surface for years. Scholars have filled libraries parsing the genealogies of hundreds of dissident groups that began to gnaw at the European empires during the period. Standard histories allege a Victorian-era "balance of power" between the European empires, but it more resembled a bar-room brawl. When they were not launching adventures to sop up the few remaining colonial lands left unclaimed in Asia and Africa, the emperors were increasingly vexed by revolutionary plots by dissidents in long-time provinces that now dreamed of nationhood. Restive outbreaks in Ireland, the Balkans, Crimea, and Arabia forced rulers to send troops that neither placated nor subdued. Soldiers consumed money that could have been better spent on other things, and also demanded a constant infusion of youth, so it should not surprise that revolution simmered most hotly in universities and in the ranks of young officers tired of official ineptitude and lost wars.

In Constantinople, the Committee of Union and Progress had begun as a secret society formed in the 1880s among the medical students of the new university in Constantinople founded by Abdul Hamid II. It soon made alliances with disaffected military cadets, whose zeal for modernizing Turkey had been kindled during the training courses they attended in Germany.

As the cadets became officers of rank they took control of the CUP and by the summer of 1908 were strong enough to launch a rebellion that forced Abdul Hamid II to give up his absolute power and restore the constitution he had banned in 1878. The rebellion supposedly installed a multiparty parliamentary monarchy bent on reform and modernism. But as the struggle for dominance continued between the CUP and other rival reform movements against the Sublime Porte, the CUP became steadily more nationalist, more centralized, and more demanding that Turkish society become more Ottoman, more Muslim, and less welcoming to other nationalities and faiths who had existed there for centuries. It did him little good, however.

Abdul Hamid II did not last another year as monarch. This

seems to be the natural order of succession among the Sultanate. He had, after all, ousted his uncle and was about to be pushed aside for his own brother. Abdul Hamid's decline had been sordid indeed. For all his reformist zeal at the start, Abdul Hamid proved mentally unstable, paranoid, and given to fits of murderous reprisals against ethnic dissidents among the empire's diverse population. He ordered the first systematic attacks on Armenian Christians, which seven years later would expand into the genocide of millions. In April 1909 he was deposed by the Young Turk hierarchy and replaced with another more pliable and even more mentally weak sibling, Mehmed V.

The doddering Mehmed V would know no peace or real power. Lands once firmly in the grip of the Ottoman Empire splintered into rebellions and a series of bloody conflicts known as the Balkan Wars. Within the walls of the Sublime Porte, the paranoia that was the inheritance of the descendants of Osman took on a political reality. The new Sultan preferred solitude so he could perfect the poems he wrote and gave over almost all real power in a further coup in 1913. With such threats outside and within its borders, the Sultan (who still was Caliph) and his military patrons in political power both despised and feared any people who were not Ottoman Turks. Ethnic cleansing became increasingly relied upon to punish and subdue.

Because of the recent centennial of the start of World War I, there has been a revived debate among historians as to the exact date that the Great War became an inevitability. For our purposes, it can be argued that that monstrous conflict had its Middle East beginnings in September 1911 when the relatively recent unified monarchy of Italy (1871) decided to reclaim part of its ancient Roman heritage by sending 34,000 troops to invade the Ottoman Mediterranean province of Libya.

There was no question of Constantinople sending an equal counterforce. Instead, a young major named Ismail Enver and a handful of "volunteer" junior officers arrived and organized a lethal guerrilla campaign using Bedouin tribesmen who were outraged by the invading nonbelievers. Using savage attacks on Italian patrols and isolated outposts, the Bedouin penned the invaders into the towns that hugged the Mediterranean coast. The success of the campaign made a national hero out of Enver and vaulted him into the top ranks of the CUP junta.

All of this turmoil was far away from Zichron Ya'akov for the time being. If anything, the upheavals in Constantinople further weakened the power of the provincial governors. As their economic situation grew more promising, the Aaronsohns built two more structures at Athlit: a greenhouse and herbarium for Aaron's plants, and a separate library and study for his books.

Sarah was now working almost full-time, cataloguing the plant specimens arriving from Aaron's trips for an herbarium at the new experiment station ten miles away. She was now nearly twenty and prospective suitors, and not just hometown lads, began to call with invitations to picnics, dances, and Sunday strolls along Founders Street. For the moment, however, Sarah was content to enjoy her physical freedom and the intellectual stimulation of aiding Aaron.

The invasion of Libya in 1911 put an end to that idyll. The guerrilla war in that far-off province added to the strain on already-straitened burdens of the Turkish military. Even as the Young Turk military commanders were consolidating their hold on the Porte, they faced perils on almost every border of the empire.

Turkey's European provinces in the Balkans were the most vulnerable. Russia was still determined to control the areas around the Black Sea. Tsar Nicholas II publicly vowed to regain

Constantinople as the historic center of Orthodox Christianity. Austria–Hungary wanted to regain one of its lost Adriatic ports for its navy. The Germans eyed ways to push a railroad through Turkey to threaten Britain's possessions in India and the Orient. And the British hung onto Egypt and the Suez Canal with fierce determination.

Then in 1912 some of the larger Ottoman vassal states rose up, each determined to achieve full independence. Sparked first by tiny Montenegro, its alliance with Serbia, Greece, and Bulgaria quickly overwhelmed the more poorly led Turkish armies and in seven months not only cost the Turks those lands but also led to an independent Albania.

This First Balkan War ended in May 1913 but Bulgaria was left feeling cheated of land it coveted. The resulting Second Balkan War began a month after the first peace treaty had been signed and lasted just short of six weeks. This time Serbia emerged as the big winner but the Young Turks (many of whom were now commanders) managed to seize back some of its border provinces and were judged by public opinion to have reclaimed national honor.

In 1913 a triumvirate of CUP generals seized personal power from the last rival faction ensconced in the Sublime Porte. Even though Sultan Mehmed V remained titular head of state, the new government they set up became known as the Three Pashas. At the head of the trio was the hero of the Libyan war, Ismail Enver, who was made Minister of War. Mehmed Talaat was the Grand Vizier over the sprawling civil bureaucracy. The third important post of Naval Minister went to a general who had a few modest successes during the Balkan wars and was now the mayor of Constantinople.

At thirty-one, Ahmed Gamal Djamal had been more successful building alliances within the CUP than he had as a commander. He became a problematic equal in the triumvirate. Very soon, Djamal Pasha would become an ominous presence in the lives of all the Jews of Palestine and a dangerous threat especially to the Aaronsohn family.

The Three Pashas immediately began to augment their power through alliances with Germany's Kaiser Wilhelm, who sent weapons and officers to modernize the army and new battleships for the now-decrepit Turkish navy. The Three Pashas also pursued a relentless program to rid the population of long-established communities of foreigners; the first targets were Greeks and Armenians who were driven from their homes, and who died by the thousands as they sought refuge elsewhere.

In Palestine the various tribal groupings of Arabs also felt the crackdown from Constantinople. Various regions of Ottoman Arabia spawned their own liberation movements, again sparked by young Arab students who had attended universities in Europe. Arrests and executions of suspect Arab leaders left it increasingly clear to the Jews of Zichron Ya'akov that they were hardly immune.

Any unified response by the Jews of Palestine never was likely. The rabbis of the old Yishuv clung to their strategy of placating Turkish authorities. They and their dependent followers still resented the early settlers, now all the more so because early *aliyots* like the Aaronsohns and others had become very prosperous in their own right—wealthy enough to send their children off for foreign educations and their wives on shopping excursions in Paris, Rome, and Berlin. New conflicts among Palestine's Jews had been further complicated by the arrival of the *Second Aliyah*. An estimated twenty thousand of these new arrivals brought with them a mix of political ideologies—varying shades of Marxist–Bolshevik theory mingled with the idealized communal philosophy fashioned late in his life by Leo Tolstoy.

What they dreamed of was jarred sharply by what they found on arrival. They sought a fertile ground for their paradise of *kibbutzim*—collective farms where everything from work to housing and to family structures would be held communally by Jews for the benefit of Jews alone. Instead, to their disgust, they found old-style villages reminiscent of the Europe they had renounced. The first *aliyots* lived in their own houses on their own land, each family responsible for its own economic welfare. Worse, some settlers did not farm at all; the prosperity of those who did enabled others to practice their traditional craft skills and to engage in commercial trade. Most offensive of all, the first generation had become dependent on labor provided from the adjacent Arab villages.

After 1912, the turmoil caused by the Young Turk revolt eroded what little official protection the Jewish communities had enjoyed. Bedouin desert raiders and, sadly, even some of their nearby Arab neighbors, used the breakdown in stability to pilfer grain and livestock and sometimes engage in wanton vandalism of Jewish farms. The more militant young arrivals in other towns and villages were quick to use Arab predations as an excuse for retaliation and increased violence under the pretext of protecting their communal *kibbutz*. For Aaron and his brothers, the increasingly vulnerable older Jewish settlements along the Mediterranean coast needed to consider how to defend themselves.

Sarah was overjoyed at Aaron's return in January 1910 from his American tour. Not only had he basked in the celebrity of his wheat discovery, but also he had won a host of new converts to the Zionist cause among prominent American Jews who had been skeptics. From them he had secured an American charter and funds for an experiment station at Athlit, and a donated windmill to raise the water needed for irrigation.

The new project gave Sarah something useful to do. While she had been away on her tour, Rivka, the younger sister, had assumed the chores of cataloguing the plants and reports that Aaron had shipped home. She was two years younger than Sarah, and a far different personality from Aaron, Alex, and Sarah. Where they were tall, robust, and competitive, Rivka was small, shy, and self-effacing. Rivka had ambitions of her own, but she suppressed whatever resentment she felt for her outsized older siblings. She would wait. Her time would come.

Sarah was glad to have her sister shoulder some of the burden of assisting Aaron. Sarah would be involved in the new project at Athlit but she also had other obligations. As the oldest daughter, she was now increasingly responsible for running the house on Founders Street. Her mother Malkah was in ill health, so the care and feeding of Ephraim and her younger brothers became her immediate duty. While Sarah was evolving into a modern personality, she still had part of her life tied to the traditional woman's role of cook, house cleaner, and mender of clothes. Malkah, after a long illness, died the next year, early in 1913, leaving Sarah in full charge of the Founders Street home and the care of Ephraim.

But life was not all drudgery. In March 1912, Sarah met a dashing young man named Absalom Feinberg, who was from Hadera. They were introduced almost as an afterthought by Aaron at a *Purim* festival dance held at the Zichron communal barn. The threshing floor had been swept spotless and trestles of food and wine drew the entire village. Sarah was now twenty-two, an age when most girls of the town had already married, but she had never found any of the young men she knew interesting enough. Absalom Feinberg was different and there was an immediate spark between them.

If the Aaronsohns of Zichron were a source of controversy to their neighbors, the Feinbergs who lived in Hadera, a day's journey to the south, were an endless source of uproar to theirs. Israel Feinberg had been one of the early *aliyots* and he had chosen the most dismal of swampy sites to locate his settlement. He argued that fulfilling the promise of Biblical Palestine's abused land demanded they work hardest at the least likely locations. He also was among the first of the new village settlers to rebel against technical overseers brought in by Baron de Rothschild from his North African plantations.

There was another trait that Israel Feinberg and his wife's family, the Belkinds, shared that set them apart from both the baron's managers and other, more orthodox fellow settlers. He admired the indigenous Arab inhabitants for their endurance and their adherence to their own religious faith. When Absalom was ten, Israel put him under the tutelage of a prominent local Arab scholar with a request not only to teach the boy Arabic but also to acquaint him with the Koran and the tenets of the Muslim faith. As a teenager, Absalom and his cousin Naaman Belkind would don Arab dress and go off on horseback adventures with their Arab friends. Some of the locals cheerfully honored him by addressing him as a sheik.

Israel sent Absalom off to France for formal education when he was fifteen. During the five years he spent abroad he attracted favorable notice in Paris as a poet. But Paris was also a capital for radical philosophers of all stripes and the young man drank deeply from these existing wells. He became an impatient convert to the rising tide of rebels against imperial tyranny sweeping Europe, and he developed a burning desire to hasten the building of a *Zion* homeland for all Jews. With the new zealotry came a fiery hatred of the Turks and their cold oppressions of every non-Ottoman inhabitant of their empire. He was a revolutionary in the making.

At first, Sarah and Absalom seemed to be made for each other. Tall and full-figured, her beauty was emphasized by her blue eyes, coppery hair, and easy laugh. There was nothing shy or hesitant about her; not for her the coy flirtatiousness of other village girls. Absalom was a year older, taller, with a muscular leanness, and dark soulful eyes that sparked fire when he spoke of his passions for Israel. Both were daring riders and crack pistol shots. Like the older Aaronsohn offspring, Absalom relished competition on horseback and swimming in the surf off Athlit. He also enchanted both Sarah and Rivka with a steady outpouring of poetry ranging from the deeply romantic to stirring calls for a rising *Zion*.

Absalom had come to Zichron Ya'akov in the wake of his father's illness and death. In Ephraim he found a surrogate who had been every bit as successful as his father. The Aaronsohns had been among the first to shift their farming from grain crops to planting extensive wine-grape vineyards. Ephraim was among the organizers of a modern wine press and bottling operation that became an important source of both the kosher sacramental wine and a popular commercial vintage that was much in demand in the booming port cities of Haifa and Jaffa.

In Aaron, Absalom found a heroic older brother to emulate. In the younger man, Aaron found the acolyte who would devote his considerable energy and skill to making his dreams for the Athlit station flourish. It was an ideal relationship. Absalom's total command of Arabic, his affection for the workers at the station, and his seeming inexhaustible energy made him an ideal manager as Athlit's experimental beds were expanded and as new reclamation projects spread on the land above the beach.

Absalom had an important impact on Aaron as well. Absalom's fierce Zionism coupled with his intolerance of any oppression visited on the Jewish settlements found an echo in Aaron.

He had always been short-tempered but in past confrontations with officials in Haifa he had opted for negotiation and compromise rather than defiance. Absalom began to convince him that such temporizing was useless. "I would set fire to the Turks as easily as I light a candle," he would dramatically declare.

Absalom quickly became a presence in the lives of all the Aaronsohns. Life was not all debate and declarations. He was clearly taken with Sarah and she with him. He spent most of his days at the Athlit station. Throughout 1913, whenever Absalom came to Zichron, he and Sarah were increasingly affectionate and easy with one another. That summer he went to Ephraim and asked for permission to wed Sarah. Then he made his proposal to her, fully expecting her acceptance.

But something held Sarah back from taking the risk of truly falling in love with this charismatic friend. Had Absalom pushed his suit with more passion, Sarah might have given her heart. Why she did not is a puzzle. At twenty-three, Sarah was five years and more past the age when other girls in Zichron Ya'akov began to marry. Plenty of young men had shown an interest, many of them had been good friends and welcome partners at the dances and parties neighbors gave. She had become a strikingly beautiful woman, glowing with vitality and spirit.

That last quality may provide a clue. Zichron Ya'akov and other parts of Palestine had flourished in the previous two decades. Haifa had become remarkably modern. Automobiles were seen on its now paved streets. There were European-style hotels, movie theaters, and a growing community of European and American businessmen. The highway to Zichron Ya'akov had been modernized so the Aaronsohns' carriage could travel there in a couple of hours rather than in a day. The village itself could be mistaken for one anywhere in Europe.

But close at hand were the wildness and uncertainty of the mountain passes where bandits lurked in the hillside caves and Bedouin raiders prowled on the outskirts of the desert beyond. Sarah had reveled in that wildness. Her horseback treks accompanying Aaron in his botanical expeditions, her pistol securely holstered to her saddle, were exhilarating. While part of her changing personality was that of the fashion-conscious modern woman, another facet was that of the dutiful Jewish daughter. Clearly, though, the streak of wild unfettered creature of the hills and desert existed too. How could she choose one role and let the others go?

Absalom Feinberg and Sarah, ca. 1914

She did love Absalom. But he could show a burst of immature reckless anger at some perceived injustice and perhaps that caused some hesitation on her part. One can also speculate that Sarah measured any prospective husband against the image of her older brother Aaron and found Absalom wanting, at least for the moment. There was pressure on her to marry, nevertheless. It was both the duty of a young woman and also an avenue to achieve the independence of her own home. But not just yet.

It was inevitable that Absalom would turn a speculative eye to Rivka. Small and delicate in contrast to her older sister, Rivka had a beauty of her own, bright red hair, a cheerful freckled face, and a quiet passivity that allowed Absalom to tease her more intimately than he would have dared with Sarah. Rivka had an agenda of her own, and why not? She was perhaps not as intellectually precocious as her older siblings but she was certainly intelligent and had a value all her own. In time even Sarah realized the focus of Absalom's attentions were drifting. It began slowly. Absalom began writing romantic teasing poems to both girls, perhaps at first to nudge Sarah into making a final decision, but it became clear that Rivka was far more welcoming of his attentions.

CHAPTER FOUR

Love and War

....

1913–1914

Sarah Aaronsohn and her husband, Chaim Abraham, in Baku, 1914

After the Three Pashas' assumption of power in January 1913, life at Zichron began to lurch from crisis to crisis and it seemed the Aaronsohns were often in the center of the turmoil. Even though Aaron had returned from his American triumph with money to build the Athlit station, he spent little time at the construction site, leaving the transfer of his plants at Founders

Street and the construction of the main station house and library to his sisters. In addition to money for the Athlit project, Aaron had secured a commitment of steady contributions from the American Zionists to provide aid to the community organizations of Zichron Ya'akov and other villages in the region.

This largesse often caused as much resentment among the recipients as it did grudging gratitude. To be fair, Aaron often was too often peremptory in the advice he offered along with the funds. He returned from one American sojourn with funds to build a fully equipped clinic for Zichron for the express purpose of finding ways to combat the malaria that was a constant health threat to the region. In choosing the clinic's director, Aaron made a mortal enemy of the village's long-time doctor, Hillel Yaffe, who had been a close friend and supporter. Doctor Yaffe had assumed he would be named director of the clinic and was shattered when Aaron imported a younger doctor from elsewhere without any thought of the impact. The fact that the younger doctor had done research on malaria counted for little with Yaffe and his supporters in the town.

Moreover, during these prewar years, Aaron was often away from Zichron so he remained unaware of the resentment that was building against him. He embarked on a seemingly endless tour of European scientific capitals and return trips to U.S. speaking venues where he entranced audiences (and newspaper reporters) with his eloquence about the potential of Palestine and the destiny of the Jewish people.

Earlier, in 1911, there also was some pointed comment when Aaron persuaded Alexander to go to the United States. News filtered back to Zichron that the twenty-three-year-old Alexander had filed the first papers needed to become a U.S. citizen and that he had been hired by Aaron's mentor David Fairchild for an important job at the Department of Agriculture. Where Aaron had won notice for his impressive command of science and his vision for Palestine, Alex (as he liked to be called in America) was a charmer and soon became popular among influential Zionists in Washington and New York.

With the same restless energy of his older brother, Alexander also began to churn out newspaper articles and magazine stories in such influential outlets as *The Atlantic Monthly* extolling the promise of Palestine and emphasizing Aaron's early comparisons between the region and the booming farm climate of California. The articles were reprinted in Europe and made their way to Zichron village. Sentiment held that one Aaronsohn celebrity swanking about abroad was enough, two was too much.

If the villagers had known about it, they would have been even more resentful at how high the Aaronsohn brothers were flying in American political circles. Both brothers had established solid contacts among wealthy Zionist supporters in Chicago and New York. Because both were frequently working with Fairchild at the U.S. Department of Agriculture building in Washington, DC, they began to circulate among a circle of ardent young American Progressives who had come to the capital to make their political fortunes.

Washington on the eve of World War I was still a small city of neighborhoods separated by the government branches they served. Just as Capitol Hill drew members of Congress, so the newly trendy Dupont Circle area in midtown was a convenient walk for those who labored at the White House, the U.S. Treasury, or the ornate Second Empire building at Seventeenth and Pennsylvania Avenue that housed the War Department, State Department, and Navy Department.

The Aaronsohns visited homes around Dupont Circle such

as the mansions of Secretary of State Robert Lansing and nephews John Foster Dulles and Allen Dulles, as well as the home of the sociable Assistant Navy Secretary Frank (as he was known then) Roosevelt. But they would have been most at home and were more frequent visitors at a bachelor's boardinghouse on Nineteenth Street that had become known as the House of Truth.

Boardinghouses offered not only rooms and meals, they also served as social centers where young men and women could gather in respectable settings according to their tastes. So there were residences for teetotalers, suffragettes, western ranchers, and others of special interests who had come to Washington to advance their causes.

As for the house on Nineteenth Street, Felix Frankfurter, who later became a Supreme Court Justice, later recalled that, "It was Justice (Oliver Wendell) Holmes who gave the place its name, the House of Truth, to tease us because we all were so certain we were right. He also said we were the brightest minds and the fastest talkers in town. And we were."

And they were. Starting in early 1913 regular residents at the House of Truth included Frankfurter and Walter Lippmann, later the most influential political commentator of mid–twentieth-century American journalism. Also in residence were two British noblemen, Lord Eustace Percy and Philip Kerr, a Scottish marquis. Both Frankfurter and Lippmann had been supporters and advisers to former President Theodore Roosevelt and his gradualist form of Progressivism. But as Germany's aggressions began to threaten America's security, they and others had shifted allegiances to Woodrow Wilson and had come for jobs in the government. Because the two British diplomats shared similar views through their brand of Fabian Socialism, the House of Truth soon became a mecca for ambitious young Progressives of both sexes.

Drawn by the all-night political debates as well as the supplies of that new cocktail, the daiquiri, and stacks of new records of that hot music called jazz, the young elitists mingled happily with Holmes, other justices, and Cabinet officers who dropped by regularly. On any given night the Aaronsohns could meet prominent figures such as Herbert Hoover, the beau ideal of the Progressives for his wartime relief efforts. The Dulles brothers, Roosevelt, and Herbert Croly, the editor of the influential magazine *The New Republic* dropped by regularly. The Danish-American sculptor Gutzon Borglum one night scrawled with a piece of charcoal across the dining room tablecloth his plans for a mammoth design that later would become the iconic Mount Rushmore memorial in South Dakota.

Aaron made his mark among these talented young strivers. He had the stature of his scientific discoveries, and he would have mesmerized fellow Jews like Frankfurter and Lippmann with his dreams of a democracy in the Mediterranean that would be a flourishing home for Jews of all nationalities to find haven. One of the frequent drop-ins, William Bullitt, then a news reporter and later an important U.S. diplomat, would say that Aaronsohn "was the greatest man I ever met."

So impressed with Aaron's dynamic presence were House of Truth regulars Frankfurter and Lippmann that they once arranged a dinner for him with former President Theodore Roosevelt. To great hilarity they watched as the normally loquacious Roosevelt was kept silent for an hour as Aaron held forth on land reclamation (a pet cause of Roosevelt's) and the future of a Zionist Palestine.

No one, not even Aaron in his most visionary mood, could foresee what awaited these youthful contacts six years later when all of them would meet again at the 1919 Versailles Peace Conference that brought an end to World War I. Percy and Kerr would be the chief foreign policy advisers to Prime Minister David Lloyd George. Hoover once again would dominate headlines with his postwar refugee relief program. Lippmann would assist Wilson in drafting his famous Fourteen Points manifesto for world peace. Frankfurter would not only serve as a wartime aide to Ambassador Henry Morgenthau but also be a leader of the American Zionist delegation to Paris to urge the creation of a Jewish state. Their eagerness to help their old House of Truth friend Aaronsohn elevated him to critical influence at that conference equaling that of the costumed pleader for Arab supremacy in the Middle East, T.E. Lawrence.

Back home in Zichron Ya'akov, Aaron's neighbors would have been dismayed to learn of these friendships in the making and what they might mean for their futures. At that moment, however, they had more pressing worries. Since Zichron had become one of the most prosperous of the old Rothschild villages, it became a natural target for the young evangelists of the *Second Aliyah* who demanded laboring jobs in the vineyards and fields in place of the Arab laborers. These young firebrands (including, briefly, David Ben-Gurion) were quite emphatic in criticizing private property ownership and urging communal decision making for the main commercial efforts—the stores, the winery, and vineyards. They made no secret that they wanted to replace the Arab laborers as a start to expelling Arab neighbors from their own villages nearby, and ultimately from Palestine itself.

These tough, new arrivals had several advantages over the earliest pioneers. Their movement had been partly sponsored and organized by the now dominant Zionist Organization founded by Theodor Herzl and Chaim Weizmann. Many of the émigrés had belonged to political parties back home such as the Polish Jewish

Socialist Workers Party, *Poalei Zion,* and they quickly formed expatriate branches in Palestine. They had a fixed ideological vision of what they wanted to create that jarred sharply against the customs of the first farmers.

Violence was inevitable. The sons of the earliest pioneers resented the swagger of the new men and mocked their often clumsy farming techniques; the newcomers sneered at the young villagers for being ignorant rustics. Fights erupted at dances. Then it got worse as Arab farmers retaliated indiscriminately against their former employers and persecutors alike. Arab watchmen who used to protect livestock and fields at night from random Bedouin pilfering now turned to stealing cows and sheep. The older Jewish farmers were at first unwilling to escalate with reprisals. The custom of the time allowed a farmer to reclaim his stolen stock in an elaborate charade where apologies and a token bribe would be offered. Not so the new arrivals who formed watch groups of their own, bolstered by arms secured from European allies.

As these clashes had increased throughout 1911 and 1912, Aaron and whatever influence he might have brought to bear was gone from Palestine. David Fairchild had secured a $300-a-year stipend for Aaron as a consultant and organized a schedule of speaking engagements in the U.S. and Canada to groups of scientists and farmers interested in the farming techniques he had put in place at Athlit.

While he was away, the elders of Zichron mistakenly put their faith in the reform pledges of the new Ottoman government to restore order. But in villages where the more radicalized new arrivals had taken control, these tough new men took matters into their own hands. Led by members of militant groups such as the Socialist-Zionists *Poale Zion* from Poland, armed groups named *Ha-Shomer* (literally, "Watchmen") began to arm themselves. At first, the *Ha-Shomer* sought only to replace the Arab guards who had protected commune flocks and crops at night. But by 1913, the groups had expanded into a defense force for the commune movement that assumed the law enforcement role of the now war-distracted Turkish government. Unsurprisingly, the Watchmen ignored the raids on Jewish villages of the early pioneers, with special scorn for towns like Zichron Ya'akov and Hadera.

The vulnerability of these towns did not last long. Early in 1913, Alexander returned from America laden with equipment to produce motion pictures and the equally popular stereopticon photographs that produced a three-dimensional picture of exotic places and major public events for home viewing. He intended to produce for American and European audiences a compelling vision that would prompt greater support for returning Palestine to its Biblical prosperity. But once he arrived he was appalled at how unsafe Zichron and the nearby villages had become.

In Absalom he found a similar impatient and reckless soul. Without Aaron being there to counsel and possibly restrain them, the two set out to organize their own defense force. Starting with young friends from Zichron, the two gathered an initial force of sixty young men from the surrounding region. They named themselves the Gideonites, after the Biblical Jewish victor over the Midianites. They differed at the start from the *Ha-Shomer*, who had first started out on foot unarmed and with the intention to use the minimum force against theft. But the Gideonites had their own horses and arms. More, they joined as a brotherhood, with a sworn oath of secrecy and a pledge to match violence done to them with greater retaliation.

Soon the Aaronsohns used contacts among the merchants

of Haifa to secure a greater stock of arms. Once the arms were secured members their initial aim was modest enough. Whenever Arab villagers harmed Jewish settlers or their property, there would be swift reprisal. Turkish protection would no longer be relied upon. But the Gideonites did not think of themselves as challengers to Turkish rule. At least not at first.

Rivka Aaronsohn

By the fall of 1913, that last autumn of peace, another dramatic change occurred. Absalom broke the impasse with Sarah and proposed to Rivka, who quickly said yes. Sarah had little chance to come to terms with Absalom's abrupt transfer of his affections. She could hardly protest, for it had been her reluctance that had driven him into her sister's arms. Just as abruptly events far away from Zichron Ya'akov began to intrude on everyone's awareness. There was so much to do and trouble was in the air.

While the Gideonites at first had been able to ward off pillagers of the village crops and livestock with warnings, confrontations began to turn more violent as Arab villages once considered friendly were themselves being squeezed by Turkish officials and found it easier to retaliate against the Jews. Alexander and Absalom were now often away getting into skirmishes with the other Gideonites, leaving Sarah to do double duty at home and at the Athlit station. Rivka and her betrothal was a vexation to be dealt with later.

In the spring of 1914, Sarah's personal life was thrown into turmoil. What prospects there might have been for love with the dynamic Absalom Feinberg had dried up before her eyes. Her hesitancy had cost her a man she had truly loved. But it was clear that Rivka loved Absalom too and it was unthinkable that Sarah would object to the new betrothal. The spark between them when they first met now must be smothered.

Absalom continued to be a permanent fixture at the Athlit station and in the Aaronsohn house in Zichron Ya'akov. He continued to be affectionate with Sarah. But Rivka now reveled in her triumph as only a younger sister can when she has spent her life in the shadow of siblings who are larger than life.

Sarah felt conflicting emotions of disappointment and relief, but now faced a serious problem. By the traditions of the time, the younger daughter in a Jewish family could not marry until her older sister was wed. But whom would Sarah marry?

Aaron offered a solution. He had a good friend in Constantinople, a wealthy merchant named Chaim Abraham. He was a pleasant man, not bad looking, a bit more than ten years older than the twenty-four-year-old Sarah. Abraham had often visited Zichron Ya'akov and had always made a good impression, so he was hardly a stranger. He also was a vocal supporter of the Zionist dream and spoke often of selling his prosperous import business and buying land to settle and develop near Zichron Ya'akov. Best of all, he wanted to marry, and his wife could look forward to a life of cosmopolitan luxury in a huge mansion in the Galata part of Constantinople. It was clearly to be an arranged marriage with no thought of romantic courtship.

Indeed, some have speculated the match was merely a sham to permit Rivka to marry Absalom, and that after a respectable period Sarah and Chaim would dissolve their marriage and she would resume her life in Zichron Ya'akov. But that speculation ignores the scandal that a divorce would ignite in the community. Sarah would be the one shamed by the community and she most certainly would never find another husband.

From left foreground: Rivka, Sarah, and Ephraim Aaronsohn.
Left middle: Alexander and Shmuel Aaronsohn, and Sarah's husband
Chaim Abraham. Rear: Aaron Aaronsohn. (March 1914)

More plausibly, the stark truth is that both Sarah and Chaim Abraham talked themselves into the match. Both wanted to marry someone suitable. Sarah liked him but certainly was not in love with the sedate, portly merchant. To Alexander, she tried a more lighthearted tone, "Rivka has written about the surprise I have prepared for you. I am glad she broke the news, for I find it hard to tell you. . . . I wish you were here to get to know the bargain I have chosen—a red-bearded Jew. How you will mock me!"

For his part Abraham saw advantages in marrying into the Aaronsohn clan, with its prosperous interests in the developing lands around and the popular winery. When he and Ephraim sat down to discuss the dowry that would be Sarah's wedding portion, Chaim at first balked at the father's offer of a large tract of land adjoining the already flourishing vineyards. He preferred cash. But he had made promises about giving up his endless travels as a merchant and settling down nearby, and Sarah clearly assumed that after a brief adventure in Constantinople she would be returning to her homeland and family with her husband. She should have been warned when Chaim accepted the land portion as dowry with some grumbling. But she went ahead anyway.

She suggested a joint wedding ceremony with Rivka and Absalom, an offer Rivka briskly refused, saying she wanted her own wedding, probably early in 1915. Chaim returned to Constantinople, supposedly to prepare to receive his new bride. She might joke with Alexander but her doubts continued, as she confessed in a letter to Aaron—who had been away when Chaim had proposed. "I must admit the whole matter seems somewhat strange—but the fated day had to come and it has arrived. I hope you like the man I have chosen—that would please me. God grant we may be happy."

Her decision to go ahead did not bar her from showing her prospective husband her hot temper when she learned that he had wrangled with her father over the dowry settlement. She wrote to him in Constantinople, "I can't understand you, Chaim. From what you told me . . . the money won't make any difference to you. So what have you, the ardent Zionist, to gain by preferring a miserable sum of money to soil drenched with the sweat of pioneers?"

Once she moved to Constantinople in March, Sarah at first wrote back enthusiastic letters about the sights and her experiences in the fabled capital spanning the divide between modern European and ancient Asian cultures.

But gradually, her letters also began to reflect both her disappointment in her married life and alarm at what she was witnessing as war fever gripped the city. The lavish lifestyle Chaim had promised turned out to be a disappointment. His home was

Sarah's wedding to Chaim Abraham (March 1914)

across the straits from the main city in the ancient Jewish quarter known as Galata, a shabby ghetto where houses were jammed together with warehouses and craft shops. Chaim also turned out to be if not exactly a miser, rather tightfisted. Sarah's new home was dark, shuttered, and full of dreary and somewhat worn furniture and fixtures.

Chaim remained pleasant but after some perfunctory attempts at lovemaking, he had shifted to a cool and patronizing distance from her. He traveled throughout Europe on business trips that often lasted for weeks. In his absence he insisted that his mother and aunts preside over the running of the household and as watchdogs over Sarah's life. Sarah, with her wealth of language skills, was further offended that the family clung to speaking the Yiddish of the ghetto, while Palestinians of her generation adopted Hebrew. Bowing to the mother's insistence that Sarah not venture out of the house unless she was accompanied by other women, she took to occasional rebellious escapes in the company of other young wives of other merchants.

On a few occasions Sarah and her new friends broke free to take ferries on shopping expeditions in the enormous covered bazaars of the old city on the Asian side of the Golden Horn. They would end the outing with a totally respectable but exciting stop for tea in the fabulously ornate lobby of the Pera Palace Hotel. This was the hotel fabled in fact and fiction as the departure place for Western travelers embarking on the Orient Express luxury train. It was there, while the hotel's orchestra played the latest popular songs from Europe and America, that Sarah got her first glimpse of a slender, almost reptilian Turkish officer as he crossed the lobby from a private dining salon. He glanced at her briefly and when she asked his identity she was informed in a hushed tone that it was Colonel Aziz Bek, the chief of Constantinople's police then under the control of one of the Pashas—a man named Ahmed Djamal. There were rumors that both Bek and his Pasha master were to be given important posts in Syria–Palestine. He would later play a crucial role in her life.

There was increasing talk of a war in Europe and troubling speculation that Turkey would become entangled. The Balkan wars had caused popular unrest and doubts. Worse, Tsarist Russia had resumed its probing of Ottoman lands around the Caspian and Black seas.

Scarcely had the villagers of Zichron Ya'akov and the rest of Palestine taken these threats seriously than the war itself burst upon them. After a brief flutter of hope that the Three Pashas would remain aloof from the conflict among the European powers, they plunged in and joined the German Kaiser and his allies on October 28, 1914.

Once Turkey entered the war, Constantinople went from a city of vibrant and cosmopolitan activity to a tense, suspicious, and repressive place. Travel outside the city now required a stack of passes obtained only after lengthy questioning by Bek's security officers. Mail was strictly censored. The letters that came from Zichron Ya'akov were not consoling. Rivka wrote of the increasing scarcity of food and other fears.

Absalom, who, it was assumed, was to marry Rivka in the spring added to Sarah's unhappiness by sending disturbing signals that he might feel some ambivalence about his choice of sisters. In one letter he wrote, "I knew a trip like yours would be a wrench that doesn't mend quickly, and that every letter would open the wound again. Perhaps time will quiet the pangs of longing. . . . "

In one, he wrote her while he was away from Zichron and used the family diminutives for her name:

> *Sarati—In spite of everything, here we are, still friends and I love you with all the strength of my heart. But you make me furiously angry, and for that you are a naughty girl, Saraleh, my darling. I would like to enjoy a quieter happiness, so I ask you to send me quickly, in a registered parcel, your little sister. We will talk about you here, I promise you, and think of you when the sun goes down. In the moonbeams we will see something of your dreaming eyes, and in the flame of the setting sun your ardent heart.*

Well aware that her brothers were in a dangerous position politically, Sarah began to send fearful warnings of the reports of the massacre of Armenians and other ethnic groups. To hide her reports she wrote in tiny letters that she then covered with large postage stamps on the envelopes. As a hint, she wrote a letter to Rivka urging her to admire "the boule"; using the French word for tree-lined boulevard, but really a pun on the Hebrew word *bul*, or stamp. Rivka's return letters also carried covert reports on the increasing peril faced by the Jews in Palestine. Then the letters from Rivka stopped coming at all.

Sarah was distraught in her isolation from her family and her home. In one letter to a sister of Absalom, she wrote, "God knows how much I hate the life I lead here. Famine reigns in Palestine and I sit here without lifting my little finger."

CHAPTER FIVE

Plagues of War and Locusts

•••••••••••••••••••••••

1915

*A team waving flags tries to push a swarm of locusts into
a trap dug into the ground, ca. 1915*

The hope for a quick resolution to the four-month-old war
in Europe faded by the start of 1915. Like most people in
the Ottoman Empire, the Three Pashas had not at first intended
to become embroiled in the conflict. Their emissaries had secretly
sounded out both the British and French for possible alliances,
but both Allies had brusquely rejected the overtures; Britain's First
Sea Lord Winston Churchill enraged the Pashas by refusing to

hand over new battle cruisers that were ready for delivery from British shipyards. One motive was that Tsar Nicholas was an ally and had ambitions for Turkish territory.

Perhaps it was inevitable that Turkey would end up being drawn in on the side of the Central Powers. Germany's Kaiser Wilhelm II had made a point of paying court to the Sultan and then the Pashas from the early days of their seizure of power. He had unsuccessfully tried in 1912 to broker a return of Libya to Ottoman control. Now he pressed the Turks to provide a needed second front against Tsarist Russia in the Black Sea region.

After the insulting British denial of the new warships the Turks had paid for, the Germans promptly sold Constantinople two brand-new battle cruisers—the *Goeben* and the *Breslau*—then sent a cadre of experienced general staff officers to direct Turkey's ramshackle army formations. The Kaiser also urged the Pashas to quickly seize Turkey's lost province of Egypt. It was a tempting idea: control of the Suez Canal would block Britain from moving vital forces from its far-flung Empire to the battle-fields of France. A quick end to the war in Europe would bring huge benefits to Turkey for being on the winning side.

Long neglected Syria–Palestine became a major theater of operations and thus a major source of crisis and challenge for Constantinople. With that mix of ignorance and arrogance that characterized so many of the three rulers' actions, the region was treated as if it were enemy territory that had to be subdued. As they began to move troops into position in the winter of 1914, their control of the region began to unravel. The Pashas' spies brought troubling rumors that Arab desert tribes in the south were planning an uprising in order to secure their grip on the holy cities of Mecca and Medina. An often chaotic shifting of Turkish Army divisions to the new Suez front was soon bolstered when each unit had a German chief of staff to impose de facto direction of operations.

Convinced of a quick German victory in Western Europe, the Three Pashas moved to clamp down on the internal threats to their rule wherever they had suspicions. Starting in early 1915, the Pashas launched genocidal attacks on the Armenians, ultimately killing an estimated one million and sending an even greater number fleeing the region. At the same time they turned their attention to Palestine with dire results for independence-minded Arabs.

Key to their oppressive policies was the firm belief in a doctrine of a Pan-Turkish society purged of the polyglot populations of other nations and other faiths; those that could not be firmly controlled were to be expelled or, if need be, exterminated. Some people such as Greeks and Bulgarians would simply be driven back to their notional homelands, while other, lesser breeds would be made to disappear by force if necessary. Arabs were to be controlled; Jews would in time vanish by whatever means.

For the moment, the fact that most of the Jewish settlements remained loyal to Constantinople spared them some of the worst brutalities and it fooled some of the elders into hoping they could survive. Even some of the new arrivals—David Ben-Gurion, now a law student in Constantinople—tried vainly to raise detachments of Jewish volunteers but the notion of arming Jews was rejected by Enver Pasha.

In January 1915 the triumvirate in Constantinople sent one of their own, Pasha Ahmed Djamal, to Damascus as both the new governor and as commander of the Ottoman Fourth Army. Djamal Pasha had been part of the earliest Armenian atrocities, where he had shown a brutal zeal. He was vain, greedy, and totally unscrupulous; he was also cunning and determined to achieve an iron grip over his sprawling province. Short in stature, he had a curvature of the spine that gave him a hunched and feral appearance, which he sought to offset by wearing ornate uniforms clustered with military medals.

The forty-three-year-old Ahmed Djamal was a toxic mix of outsized ambition, ruthlessness, and startling incompetence that would prove a major contribution to the ruling triumvirate's ultimate defeat during the war. When the Three Pashas had seized power, Djamal was made Minister of the Navy, but he did nothing to resurrect that decayed force. He so stridently opposed the purchase of the two battle cruisers from the Germans that Enver Pasha maneuvered him out of the Navy Ministry, briefly making him mayor of Constantinople, and then pushing him farther away with the lure of the governorship of Syria–Palestine and the command of an entire army there.

Enver might not have done so if he had been aware that during Turkey's secret offers to France in the weeks before the war, Djamal had made a secret offer of his own: to guarantee French possessions in Syria–Palestine in return for making him ruler of the region. Later, during the war, Djamal would make a similar offer to the British: to let Britain's forces in Egypt seize control of the region, again, with Djamal as ruler of both Syria–Palestine and Egypt. The British seriously considered the offer but finally judged he was too untrustworthy for them to control.

Although a German general named Kress von Kressenstein was assigned to actually direct operations of the twenty-thousand-man Fourth Army, Djamal Pasha routinely interfered with strategic planning and diverted troops to round up more than one hundred Arab political leaders whom he suspected of fomenting the revolt that had broken out in the southern deserts. He assigned the duty of ferreting out suspect Arab leaders to his chief torturer

Aziz Bek, a colonel who was chief of his intelligence service. Bek exceeded his master in the studied art of cruelty. The young Arab leaders were rounded up, imprisoned, and tortured by Bek's interrogators in an ordeal that ended eighteen months later in a round of public hangings in Beirut in August, 1916.

At first, the entrance of Turkey into what first had appeared to be a strictly European war confused everyone in Syria–Palestine. Many of the inhabitants who were Christians had ties to either British or French trading partners. The *Second Aliyah* Jews had experienced firsthand the anti-Semitic prejudices of the Germans and of Austria. Among the older, more established Jewish residents there was the complication that they held Turkish citizenship, which they hoped would insulate them. At first, even Alexander Aaronsohn went into the army hoping that by his example Jews could escape the hostilities that the authorities were now visiting on their Arab neighbors.

In the meantime, the Pasha's troops swept throughout Syria–Palestine, seizing the resources and manpower he needed to support the Fourth Army buildup in that region. Travel within the region now required passes, mail from abroad was censored, and carts and draft animals were seized. Almost at once a tight naval blockade was imposed by the French and British navies and this cut off Palestine's burgeoning export sales of wine and citrus to European and Russian importers. Worse, the blockade cut off imports of gasoline and diesel fuel that powered the irrigation pumps that crops depended upon.

Then the Turks came after the province's young men. Jewish and Arab youths, including Alexander Aaronsohn and Absalom Feinberg, were conscripted into the army and at first many went willingly; they were, after all, Turkish citizens, and the bitter memory of Libya's seizure by British and French ally Italy still rankled. But the cooperative spirit among Palestinians of all faiths quickly vanished in the face of Djamal's depredations. While the Turks showed a brutal zeal in their confiscations, much of what they seized was so mismanaged as to be of little use to them— many of the livestock perished from neglect while crops rotted from poor storage at army depots.

For the first few weeks conscripted Christian draftees and Jews like Alexander did not face the unendurable conditions that Arab recruits did during their basic training. Because they could get money from home they could bribe their officers to get better food, cleaner uniforms, and shelter, and they also adapted more easily to the rigid training regimen now imposed by German officers. That abruptly changed when Djamal began to exercise greater control as commander. The Christians and Jews were stripped of their weapons and uniforms and moved from their training regiments to forced labor battalions where they were set to the grueling tasks of improving the roads and fortifications needed for the imminent invasion of the Suez Canal. The work was exhausting, the tools inadequate, and their rations were barely enough to keep them alive. Some way of escape had to be found.

Aaron was appalled at the abrupt turn of events. He not only feared for his brother, he also had reason to suspect the Turks would loot Athlit despite it having been accepted by Constantinople as an accredited American establishment. He sent an urgent telegram to David Fairchild in Washington asking for help in protecting the Athlit station from plundering by the Turks. Fairchild consulted Paul Warburg, now the first chairman of the new Federal Reserve central bank. The central banker worked through the U.S. State Department to arrange for the admiral in charge of the U.S. Navy's Mediterranean fleet to send a ship to rescue Aaron and his collections.

American–Turkish relations during World War I were beyond complexity. The United States never formally declared war with Turkey—even after America entered on the side of the Allies in the spring of 1917. As early as 1915, the Pashas' German advisers had strongly urged the Turks to do nothing that might lure America into the conflict. Despite an effective Anglo–French blockade of all major Ottoman ports, the American fleet in the Mediterranean was grudgingly allowed through the cordon and even more grudgingly allowed by the Turks to enter the major ports of Syria–Palestine to help rescue the hundreds of American missionaries, teachers, and merchants whose operations had been abruptly closed. Not only did this mean there was a small window of escape for Aaron and his friends but it was also the means by which the Zionist money could continue to flow into Palestine.

Back in Washington there was understandable anger when Aaron refused to be rescued and instead, in February, asked for another interview with Djamal Pasha. The rejection was put down to his reputed arrogance and lack of gratitude. However, the incident may better be explained as a case of bad communications between the State Department and its diplomats abroad. Aaron unwittingly caused the confusion when he directly appealed to his friend Fairchild in Washington and also to a new friend, America's ambassador to the Pashas, Henry Morgenthau.

The New York financier had been an early recruit of young Democrat Progressives like Bernard Baruch and Franklin Roosevelt who pushed the 1912 presidential candidacy of Woodrow Wilson. His reward was the ambassadorship. Morgenthau was much taken by his belief that he had special influence with Enver and Talaat Pasha as many of his predecessors had had with the Sultans. He had been a frequent visitor to Zichron Ya'akov and admired Aaron. His mandate as he saw it was to back President Wilson's firm determination to remain neutral in this European war. Not only was Wilson pressed by the large Irish and German constituencies of the Democratic Party, but he also cherished his conviction that he could by the moral force of his personality bring the Allies and the Central Powers to an equable peace. Crucial to this strategy was a plan advanced by Morgenthau to convince the Turks to abandon their risky alliance with the Germans and Austrians. Diplomacy and conciliation would not only convince the Pashas to drop out of the war, it would also temper their depredations against the Jews in Palestine. Aaron was a key to pacifying the new governor in Jerusalem. Or so both Morgenthau and Aaron hoped.

Pasha Djamal had dismissed with insults the first petitions for relief from other Jewish delegations. But (to the irritation of his rivals) he agreed to see Aaron. After Aaron made his arguments, Djamal slyly mused aloud, "I ask myself, what would you say if I ordered you to be hanged?" Aaron, who had for some time struggled to keep his weight manageable replied, "What should I say, Your Excellency? The weight of my body would break the (hanging) tree and the noise would be heard in America."

Luckily, Djamal laughed and he took the point. The war in Europe had converted large numbers of wealthy American Jews to the Zionist cause and a committee had been formed to send vitally needed funds to a council of Jewish leaders representing the Palestinian villages. However—and this was an important point—Aaron Aaronsohn had been given veto power over how the council distributed those funds. Most of the council wanted the funds spent directly to aid various communities, but Aaron demanded that a portion of the money be used to bribe Turkish officials for various concessions—and Djamal counted on his share. Aaron also spent some of the funds to free Alexander and Absalom from perishing in the labor battalions.

The relations between Aaron and Djamal abruptly improved a few weeks later, just on the eve of the Turks' planned attack on Suez. Early in January of 1915 an infestation of locusts had begun in the faraway southern part of Sudan. By February, just as the Turkish attack was launched, the locusts swept north in a cloud over the arid Sahara and they alighted on the green valleys of Syria–Palestine. The region had suffered locust infestations before, but not in living memory had such a disaster loomed. The insects were of the largest variety and their voracious appetites devoured every living thing in their expanding path. Crops in the fields and even the bark from trees were stripped. Vulnerable livestock were killed and devoured, and there were reports that infant children had been attacked by swarms. A greater peril would come if the females were able to plant their eggs in the soil, setting up repeated infestations of the plague.

Pasha Djamal was frantic. More Ottoman divisions were arriving to support the assault on the British; the stockpiles of grain and the crops being planted for the coming year had to be protected at all costs. Convinced of Aaron's expertise, Djamal Pasha commanded him to organize the means to halt the infestation in its tracks before it reached the coastal farm belt. Aaron told him the only effective counter to this plague was to construct an enormous network of ditches and then to literally rake the locusts by the hundreds of thousands into those ditches where they could be set on fire with gasoline. It would take an enormous effort and more manpower than the settlers themselves could muster, especially since so many were already conscripted elsewhere.

To Aaron's surprise, the governor put him in charge of organizing the regional attack on the locusts. Aaron, along with the recently freed Absalom and Alexander, quickly realized this new opportunity to advance the cause of a Jewish nation. The intelligence they could gather while working inside the three Ottoman Army groups in the region—the order of battle, the size and number of weapons and equipment, and especially hints as to the plan of the Turks' attack on Suez—would be of vital importance to the British planners in Cairo.

While Aaron continued to cling to his mistaken belief in his influence with Djamal, he had come to realize that a German victory in Europe would be a disaster reaching as far as Zichron Ya'akov and its inhabitants. Moreover, Aaron was aware that at the very start of the war the British government of Prime Minister Herbert Asquith had begun actively considering supporting a Jewish state in Palestine if Turkey were defeated. Surely an active help in the war effort by Jews would ensure England's gratitude.

While still in Jerusalem negotiating with Djamal, Aaron wrote to Alexander and Absalom a call to action. "Everybody in whose eyes freedom is precious now has to risk his life in the war against the Germans. For if, God forbid, we allow them to emerge as the victors, there will not be a single corner left in the world where we shall be able to live a life worthy of the name." They organized a new structure to carry out this task. The old Gideonite group was quickly enlisted and under the guise of fighting the locusts they began to gather information on the state of the Fourth Army that could be of great value to the British planners in Cairo.

Neither the Gideonite spy group nor the battle against the locusts gained much traction at first. When the Turkish attack on Suez came in late January of 1915, the British were able to use their advance warnings to shift the bulk of their force to the main attack points and repulse Djamal's troops with heavy losses. Among other consequences, the troops that might have been used to destroy the insects were never delegated, and Arab community leaders considered the infestation one of divine inevitability and refused to help. In April, Aaron resigned in protest, believing that he alone among Palestine's Jewish leaders had a unique ability to influence the Pasha and stave off any serious persecution of the community.

At this point Aaron was playing a double game. While Alexander and Absalom used the locust campaign to recruit more operatives throughout Palestine and bring a growing flow of intelligence to the Athlit station, Aaron continued to pay court to Djamal. For his part, the Pasha continued to grant Aaron unique access and favors that no other Jewish leader could match. But as history would prove, his determination to visit the same Armenian horrors on the Jews of Palestine merely lay dormant.

Whatever the outcome might be, Aaron realized if he was to have any role in making *Eretz Israel* a reality he needed to find a way to establish contact with the British and inform them what the Gideonite network could offer.

Djamal Pasha's attack on Suez had been a shambles from the start. The entire Fourth Army had set out in a disorganized forced march that left broken vehicles, dead livestock, and faltering troops in a trail behind them. Despite the confiscated stocks of food, Djamal's soldiers had not been provided with enough rations and many troops never reached their assigned attack points.

While the British force in Egypt was outnumbered, they were amply forewarned by their newly utilized weapon, the reconnaissance airplane, and were able to move enough troops along the Canal to repulse the Turkish attack, routing the Fourth Army. The soldiers fled back to Palestine, looting and vandalizing Arab and Jewish villages on the way. Djamal, in a rage, laid the blame on saboteurs and spies who had betrayed his plans, and there was no doubt in his mind that the heart of the betrayers lay among the Jews.

Djamal ordered all the watchmen groups—the Gideonites, the *Ha-Shomer,* and others—to turn in their guns. At first most settlements turned in some weapons and buried the rest. But Arab informers prompted the Pasha to order the arrest of suspects among young Jewish men, Alexander and Absalom among them. They were beaten and when they would not reveal where their arms were cached, the Turks threatened execution. When the prisoners remained obdurate, Djamal warned village elders in suspect communities that he would round up selected young women and imprison them in the brothels designated for officers.

The Pasha's crackdown on the Jews prompted their Arab neighbors to seek advantage against these more prosperous intruders. Dr. Hillel Yaffe was accompanying a neighbor's daughter back to the village when his carriage was attacked by a band of Arab youths. The girl was assaulted and when Yaffe tried to protect her, he was savagely beaten. Even though Rivka stayed close to the home on Founders Street, her family feared for her.

While Aaron was still safe because of his campaign against the locusts, other Gideonites had to make themselves scarce. Absalom went into hiding along with others. There were hints to Aaron that Alexander too was increasingly suspect. During a visit to Damascus to see Aaron, who was at Djamal's headquarters for the locust campaign, Alexander boldly told the Pasha that one of his trusted military commanders had been pilfering equipment and rations; the man was too important for Djamal to interfere and he made it clear he resented the embarrassing disclosures.

Sometime in May 1915, Aaron made arrangements for Alexander and Rivka to journey north by donkey to Beirut;

ever-watchful neighbors were told she was to be enrolled in an American college for safety. With Alexander wearing his old army uniform, they trudged through police checkpoints posing as a married couple. But the real goal was to reach Cairo to offer the band's services to prompt a quick British invasion of Palestine. Their chance came when a cruiser from the neutral U.S. Navy called at Haifa to take refugees who had secured visas from the Turks to go to Cyprus. Armed with false passports, Alexander and Rivka got on board and sailed.

Of a slighter build than his older brother, Alexander Aaronsohn was a charming, light-hearted personality who shared Aaron's zeal for causes but not his deliberate nature. He assumed that once he reached Cairo the British High Command would welcome the offer of the Gideonite's intelligence and use it to hasten the liberation from the Turks of what would by right become the Jewish homeland.

There were now thirty of Aaron's spies spread throughout Palestine and they had gathered a detailed list of the Turkish outposts on the Palestine coast as well as likely landing sites where a large British invasion could easily gain a firm foothold that would catch the Turks off guard. Under the guise of fighting the locusts, Aaron's recruits had observed not only the location of specific Turkish regiments, but the state of their training and equipment. Roads and bridges had been mapped along with the fortifications that German engineers were building to resist the expected British line of attack on the coastal cities. Aaron was right that, beyond the range of British scout planes, the Cairo planners had no accurate maps and no reliable agents of their own.

When they finally arrived at Alexandria in early August, British authorities at first refused Alexander and Rivka permission to land since they had Turkish passports. But friends from prewar days who had settled in Egypt intervened and at last they were able to find rooms in Cairo's Continental Hotel. By coincidence this was the same place where officers of the newly founded Arab Bureau—including a young lieutenant named T.E. Lawrence—were billeted.

Not only were Alexander and Rivka shunned socially at the Continental, but he was denied any appointments with senior planners. With characteristic impudence, Alexander began to submit articles to the English language newspaper in Cairo—the *Egyptian Gazette*—that asserted the general weaknesses of the Turkish Army, the impact of the locust plague, and the disaffection of much of the Palestinian population. The articles had the desired effect.

On August 18, Alexander went to British Army headquarters in the luxurious Savoy Hotel. There he had the bad luck to be passed over to a Major Stewart Newcombe. The meeting was a disastrous encounter where Alexander's blithe self-confidence collided with the British High Command's muddled strategy in the Middle East. The Army's top commander was a general named Archibald Murray who had a reputation for being what the British called "a safe pair of hands." Murray was a meticulous planner and organizer and had managed to turn back Djamal's attack earlier in the year. He was not only risk averse but now he faced a double problem. A substantial part of his troop strength was diverted to a massive amphibious attack on the Dardanelles passage into the Black Sea that was to launch in just two weeks—at a death trap known forever as Gallipoli. At the same time London demanded that he and his remaining troops along the Suez increase pressure on the Turks in the Saudi Arabian desert region dominating the coastline of the Canal on the eastern side.

The British Arab strategy was a mix of wishful thinking, ignorance, and facile logic. Lacking even rudimentary intelligence about the state of the Turkish forces in Syria–Palestine, the government in London had turned to Oxford's leading scholar on the region, D.G. Hogarth of the Ashmolean, and he had turned to colleagues who had experience exploring and digging at various ancient sites. These were given military rank and shipped out to Cairo to advise General Murray. Among the anointed experts were Stewart Newcombe, Leonard Woolley, and perhaps the most genuine expert on the topic, Gertrude Bell—later known as the Desert Queen, and lastly, the Mother of Iraq. After a period of idle confusion, the group in early 1915 was to be formally organized as the Arab Bureau, with Newcombe as its first head. Last to arrive was one of Hogarth's protégés, T.E. Lawrence. Lawrence had tried to join the army at the outbreak of the war but was turned out for being too short. Now he was a newly minted lieutenant but, true to this new persona-in-the-making, he insisted on wearing a mixed costume of school blazers, military gear, and Arab slippers. Newcombe kept him out of sight writing regional handbooks for operational commanders.

More important than the briefing books on local geography, the Arab Bureau's task was to devise a plan for General Murray to make use of the desert Arab tribes that occupied huge swaths of the Arabian Peninsula held by the Ottoman armies on the other side of the Suez Canal. The most likely convert was the Grand Sharif Hussein who nominally was the guardian of both Mecca and Medina, the two holiest of homes of Islam. Not only did Turkish forces hold both cities, but Hussein had evidence the Ottomans intended to depose him and replace him with a more pliable Arab sheikh, so ally Germany could have a clear field to build its strategic railroad all the way to the Arabian Gulf and threaten India.

Once she too was in Cairo, Hogarth and Newcombe relied on Bell—who held a vague rank of political officer—for her decades of experience in the region and her personal friendship with Hussein. The Sharif needed propping up from the start for although he feared the Turks, his own forces were poorly armed and untrained as a coherent military force against even the ramshackle Ottoman armies. He would need guns, advisers, and, most of all, huge sums of gold to win the loyalty of other tribal leaders.

So Newcombe had his hands full, for his staff had such a diversity of opinions as to which specific Arab leaders should be supported. Hussein had a number of sons, each of whom led sizable forces, but not all of whom were likely to back their father. The one point of universal agreement within the Arab Bureau was that the Jewish settlements of Palestine were of no consequence. A residue of endemic prejudice against Jews that infected many Britons of that time arguably had its impact as well.

The major was immediately suspicious of this plausible young man Alexander Aaronsohn, who was both a Turkish citizen and a Jew. When Newcombe asked him what money this supposed band of spies would need, Alex mistakenly thought he would enhance his proposition by refusing any compensation. That merely made Newcombe more abrupt. Moreover, Alex was distressed to learn that the London government planners had already dismissed Palestine as a theater of operations. Djamal Pasha's attack, as disastrous it had been for the Turks, had convinced the British that a counterattack was too risky to attempt at that moment. A coastal landing was out of the question.

Instead, top officials in London (prompted by First Lord of the Admiralty Winston Churchill) had pointed to Gallipoli as the keystone of their strategy. It was the kind of ornate scheme beloved by war planners operating at a distance from reality. The plan was a bid to open passage into the Mediterranean for the Russian Navy, which was penned up in the Black Sea.

One key factor in the doomed attempt to force their way through the heavily fortified straits of the Dardanelles was the hope that opening the straits would help their embattled Russian allies and could bring still-ambivalent Bulgaria and Greece onto the Allied side. That implausible logic, however, was undone by a mix of ignorance about the state of Turkish defenses on the peninsula and blithe assumptions about the abilities of the Allied forces that would actually have to carry the battle. There was not, for example, a single up-to-date study of the Ottoman Empire in the library of the British Foreign Office. What Asquith's planners knew about Gallipoli came from vague reports from journalists, missionaries, and business travelers. Tragically, the plan drafted by First Lord of the Admiralty Winston Churchill placed unwarranted faith in the ability of Royal Navy offshore guns to cover the untried Australian and New Zealand regiments that were to force an amphibious landing and capture the Turkish emplacements that bristled with artillery.

The Gallipoli campaign began on April 25, 1915, and would drag on until the last survivors were evacuated the next January. It was a clear disaster for the Allies, with 53,000 dead out of 250,000 total casualties of wounded or disabled—many of them from the epidemics of disease that swept through the ill-sheltered poorly supported ranks. But there could have been some comfort, had their intelligence been adequate, if the British planners in London and Cairo knew that the Turks had suffered 68,000 killed out of 300,000 casualties that could not be replaced as easily as were their forces in Egypt. Even with the Gallipoli losses, the British commander in Cairo, Lt. Gen. Archibald Murray, could boast a force of 13 divisions amounting to a mix of 400,000 troops, most just arrived from India and the volunteers from Australia and New Zealand known as ANZACs.

Turkish photographs of Gallipoli battle (April 1915)

That Gallipoli was one of the great disasters in British military annals was realized at once. Less understood at the time was the irreparable damage the Turks suffered as well. To replace the huge number of casualties they had suffered at Gallipoli, Constantinople shifted whole regiments and weaponry from the three armies strung out on the Syria–Palestine theater of operations. But the Allied commanders in Cairo would not know that for months because they would not listen to Alexander. Newcombe brusquely dismissed Alexander and later urged him to leave Cairo before he got into trouble.

Disconsolate, Rivka and Alexander managed to book passage to Cyprus in early September and went through the frustration of getting to America, where they would seek aid from their backers in the Zionist movement. There was little hope that they could slip back into Palestine. They were marooned for weeks until they could get money from America for their passage to New York.

Once they reached New York the brother and sister faced daunting prospects. Even though Alex and Aaron had made many friends during earlier trips, the mood in America in 1915 was overwhelmingly against the United States having any involvement with either side in the horrifying struggle being waged in the trenches of France. Friends like Felix Frankfurter and others from the House of Truth circle would back President Wilson's reelection campaign in 1916, which promised, "He kept us out of War."

America's Jewish community was sharply divided. Many of the wealthier class had been skeptical of the Zionist movement from the start; they had assimilated, and demands for a separate Jewish state looked provocative and doubtful. Moreover, many American Jews had family and business ties in Germany or Austria–Hungary and few had any affinity for the British. These doubters along with large Irish and German voting blocs were the base of Wilson's Democrat party. And after all, if a Zionist leader like Chaim Weizmann refused to publicly side with the Allies lest he jeopardize his patrons among the Central Powers, why should they get involved? Turkey's murderous atrocities against the Armenians was deplored and the plight of Palestine's Jewish settlements was concerning, but what could one do?

Alex turned to his considerable journalistic skills and throughout 1915 churned out articles for leading publications that sought to fuel outrage against the Turkish genocide of the Armenians and accuse the Germans of supporting the rampage. British press baron Lord Northcliffe, owner of the influential *Daily Mail*, had become head of Britain's propaganda ministry. He commissioned Alex to collect the articles and edited them into book form for distribution not only in Britain and the United States, but in foreign language editions that circulated elsewhere in continental Europe, including a clandestine issue inside Germany. *With the Turks in Palestine,* which recounted Alex's brutal experience in the Turkish Army along with the extermination of Christians, Jews, and the Armenians, was a best-seller.

All throughout 1915 Sarah languished in Constantinople. She had no way of knowing that Alex and Rivka were headed to America or that, in a characteristic burst of impatience, Absalom had defied Aaron and set out for Cairo as well, arriving there just six days after Alex and Rivka had sailed away in failure.

Finally, in the late autumn of 1915, during one of Chaim's lengthy business trips to Berlin, Sarah had had enough. A man from Zichron Ya'akov was going home and agreed to travel with her as protection. She managed to bribe her way to obtain the needed exit papers and train tickets to journey home. She left a letter for Chaim promising to return, then set out. It was a hellish three-week journey just to get to Haifa. Even when trains had once run on time, it was a lengthy trip. But now the journey was disrupted by delays and cancellations that required travel in carts over mountainous paths to reach connections.

Along the way Sarah was stunned to see whole villages that once belonged to Armenian farmers completely destroyed with piles of corpses stacked along the rail lines. What she was witness to was the first modern genocide of an estimated million and a half Armenian men, women, and children, a crime still not acknowledged by Turkey's government.

Turkish troops stopped the trains to search for targeted ethnic victims, who were dragged outside and shot within sight of the other passengers before the trains were allowed to continue. When she had to travel through mountain villages in a cart or carriage, she encountered Armenians survivors near starvation who told her horrible tales of rape and massacre. She arrived home in mid-December in exhausted shock.

She faced even greater alarm when she understood the peril the Jewish settlements had come under in her absence.

Chapter Six

Success and Setback

•••••••••••••••••••••••••••

1915–1917

Absalom Feinberg, ca. 1915

Absalom Feinberg became increasingly restless through the summer of 1915, after Alexander and Rivka had sailed for Cairo. He was forced to stay in hiding, usually in the mountain caves between Zichron Ya'akov and the desert. He missed Rivka, and now Sarah's letters had stopped arriving from Constantinople.

He most hated being forced into idleness. Whenever he managed to slip into the relative safety of the Athlit station he found Aaron absent, either overseeing his campaign against the locusts or organizing another branch of the Gideonite spy group within the Ottoman armies. Not aware that Alexander and Rivka had been stymied at British Army headquarters and would shortly leave, Absalom tried to join them in Cairo. By luck, through the Gideonite network operating in the port town of Tyre, he learned that a small French warship would pause offshore to unload support for its own sparse spy network before proceeding to Port Said in Egypt for refueling. He managed to slip aboard. He arrived six days after Alexander and Rivka had sailed for Cyprus.

Absalom had better luck than they in Egypt. Instead of trying to make contact in Cairo, he found a relative who had migrated to Egypt at the outbreak of the war and then joined the famed Zionist Mule Corps, which the British had raised among Jewish refugees there to support the fight at Gallipoli. The cousin, who was back in Egypt recovering from wounds from the battle, had made friends with one of Hogarth's younger pet archaeologists named Leonard Woolley. From 1911 through 1913, Woolley and T.E. Lawrence had spent seasons digging at the vast Mesopotamian abandoned city of Carchemish, near enough to the site staked out by Gertrude Bell to cause squabbles. Woolley had been made a Royal Navy lieutenant and installed in their separate intelligence headquarters at Port Said. Instead of renewing the offer of the Gideonite intelligence to skeptical British Army planners in Cairo, Absalom made his offer to Woolley. When Absalom revealed what the network was capable of doing, the young lieutenant eagerly passed him up the chain of command where the senior Navy staff responded with a guarded interest that was at least more willing than the Cairo planners.

Absalom was so excited by even the cautious welcome he

received, he failed to pay as much attention as he should have to the warnings Woolley and others made. There would be contact made with Athlit and the information would certainly be of interest. But it was made clear enough, if Absalom had listened closely, that an all-out liberating invasion of the Palestine coast was not immediately on the agenda. It had already been decided that the Allies would challenge Turkey at what seemed a far more strategic objective. The freedom of a handful of Jewish villages had no place in that agenda.

If British strategy appears muddled in the early conduct of World War I, especially in the Middle Eastern theater, it is largely because the British political elite were themselves in turmoil. In the autumn and winter months of 1914–1915, the Liberal Party government led by Herbert Asquith in London still toyed with their attempts, and those of the French, to bribe the three Pashas to stay out of an alliance with Germany and then later to drop out of that alliance. Other than that, the immediate goal for the Middle East was to hang onto control of Egypt and the Suez Canal as a vital supply route so troops from across the Empire could be rushed to France where the war was to be won or lost.

At first neither Aaron at Athlit nor Absalom in Egypt grasped what the ongoing debacle meant for their hopes of a liberated Palestine. They still clung to the notion that Palestine was a soft target where the British could come ashore almost anywhere along the long largely unfortified coastline and catch the Turks off-guard. In his enthusiasm for the friendly treatment he received from Woolley, Absalom ignored the implications in the questions he was asked. Could the Gideonites establish a network of coast watchers to help enforce the Allied blockade? Of course they could. Would Absalom help organize a regular schedule of transfers of all the Gideonite information about Turkish naval plans, especially any news about the Turkish battleships that were penned up at Constantinople? Certainly. And would the Gideonite intelligence on the Ottoman armies also be handed over to the navy, a real finger in the eye of the army staff in the ongoing inter-service rivalry? Again, Absalom enthusiastically agreed.

A hastily organized system of contacts was arranged where a British ship would pause in its blockade patrolling on nights of the full moon, and look for a signal from the Athlit station—open shutters on the station's seaside windows—and send a boat ashore to transfer funds and new orders in exchange for sacks of intelligence documents. In return, Woolley promised that the NILI organization would be provided with the logistics needed for a proper stream of communications. Code books and, vitally important, a small supply of British gold sovereign coins were supplied to support the spy operations but also provide aid to the straitened villagers of Zichron and other communities where Aaron had friendly relations. The last aid money from America, a generous contribution of $5,000, had come in November the year before the Allied blockade, and Turkish censorship had shut down the flow.

One can only imagine how triumphant Absalom felt when, two months after his arrival in Egypt, he was dropped off on November 8 onto the beach below the Athlit station in the dead of night with his gold and a list of specific intelligence questions for the network. He surprised Aaron at the station and swaggered just a bit with his tale of how he had been able to do what Alexander had failed to accomplish. They quickly organized the coast watchers the British wanted, and assembled an impressive set of intelligence documents about the Ottoman armies that could not fail to impress their new patrons.

For the final weeks of 1915, the spy network flourished and a steady stream of information flowed back to Athlit. But neither

Absalom nor his navy handlers had the foresight to anticipate how to keep the contacts open if unforeseen changes were to occur. It was inevitable that the British blockade schedules would be changed. The ship that was the communications link, a motorized yacht named the *Managem,* had been seized at the start of the war and was also put to use scouting along the Palestinian coast for Turkish warships. The captain was bitterly resentful about having the added duty of heaving-to so close to the shore whenever the moon was bright enough, and then waiting while messengers were rowed in and back to him on what seemed a risky enterprise at best. There was the danger of mines that the Turks had scattered without pattern along the shoreline, as well as the risk of artillery fire if they were spotted. So when navy signals were changed, the messenger sent ashore was warned not to wait, and once ashore he panicked and was rowed back without making contact. The old signal system between ship and shore no longer functioned and the *Managem's* captain was in no mood to double-check if the message had been received. Aaron and Absalom were alarmed when they stood on full moon nights watching the *Managem* pass by without responding. What had happened? Had Woolley doubted Absalom or had the navy operation been cancelled by the Arab Bureau?

At the end of December Absalom's impatience got the better of him. He resolved to go to Egypt once more to reestablish contacts. This time he would slip across the Gaza desert to a British outpost on the Suez side. He could use his Turkish uniform and passes as a locust inspector to get by the Ottoman guard posts and then rely on his skills to avoid the fierce Bedouin tribes roaming the wasteland beyond.

Despite Aaron's express orders to stay put, he set out—unaware that at that same time, Sarah was on her arduous return to Zichron

Ya'akov from Constantinople and her marriage. Riding a camel and dressed in a Turkish officer's uniform, Absalom skirted the formidable Turkish police desert outpost at the oasis town of Beersheba and was within sight of British forward positions at Katia when a Bedouin band recognized him and dragged him back to the authorities. On his way to captivity Absalom managed to tear off his officer rank buttons and swallow the small paper packet of intelligence.

Once in custody, Absalom tried to convince the Turkish gendarmes that he was a locust inspector under the mandate of no less than Djamal Pasha. The fact that he was caught far away in the desert reaches well beyond the infestation could not plausibly be explained, but he stuck to his tale. The German officers stationed at the outpost wanted to hang him at once but the Turks were uncertain. That he had official credentials in his possession worried them, so they turned to the only remedy they knew; they alternated harsh beatings with periods of intense questioning followed by periods of isolation.

The Turks, also true to form, could be bribed. Getting free was impossible, but it was customary to allow prisoners to obtain supplies of food from relatives to supplement the starvation rations that Turkish prisons provided. So Absalom used the money he had to pay for a message to reach a cousin in southern Palestine to come to his aid. Instead, the message went to a former Gideonite friend of Absalom named Josef Lishansky who lived in the southernmost Jewish settlement of Ruhama. Like Absalom, Lishansky had become an acquaintance of the Bedouin and so had free passage into the desert as far as Beersheba. He arrived with loaves of bread for Absalom and more money for the jailers to guarantee free access to the prisoner. He was able to leave the prison with new letters for Absalom's cousin and for Aaron, explaining his peril but promising to stick to his story even though it cast some suspicion on Aaron; that could not be helped.

Lishansky finally made contact with Absalom's cousin Naaman Belkind, who lived in the oldest of the Rothschild villages, a southern wine-producing competitor of Zichron called Rishon-le-Zion. Naaman supervised the wine cellars there and was the Gideonite's operations chief in south Palestine. He was a genial personality and had used generous gifts of wine to the Turkish officers stationed at Rishon to establish friendships and gather crucial information for Athlit to put into its ciphered trove for the British. Naaman easily recruited Josef into the ranks of the Gideonites and relied on him to keep Absalom supplied with food and encouragement, while he set off for Athlit to inform Aaron.

Time was crucial. The Turks could at any time lose patience trying to extract information from Absalom, and hang him. Aaron knew that a direct appeal to Djamal Pasha would be abruptly rejected. But a delegation of village elders had been summoned to Damascus by the governor on agriculture matters; Aaron inserted himself in the group. As expected, Djamal gave brief attention to the Jewish complaints and asked Aaron to prepare a survey of the problem. Aaron said he was unable to do the work because the Germans had jailed his secretary Feinberg in Beersheba and were about to hang him. Djamal had come to despise the Germans both because of their insulting attitude toward him, and because they were under the control of Enver Pasha as Minister of War and could not be countermanded when they gave orders. He could not free Absalom by direct decree so he sent a telegram to Constantinople asking Enver to direct that Absalom be brought to trial at once so he could return to a vital task back in Palestine. Three weeks after he was caught, the Turks in Beersheba finally gave up and set him free.

In the meantime, Sarah had arrived unexpectedly in Zichron Ya'akov but Aaron had deliberately not told her that Absalom was in prison or that the Gideonites had been set to spying. Although she sensed something was amiss, at first she did not press matters. She was relieved to be home at last from her frightful journey and to be reunited with her lonely father and the familiar surroundings of her home on Founders Street.

Aaron and others could not help noticing a change in Sarah's personality. She had always matched her brothers in the strength of her character and her determination. Now the atrocities she had seen on her journey and the harsh realities faced by the Jewish settlements in Palestine had ignited a fire in her soul. She now matched Absalom's fervor and militancy. Coincidentally, Aaron too was undergoing his own change in outlook.

Then, suddenly, Absalom was back, bearded, bruised, and scrawny from his ordeal but bouncing and full of irrepressible good humor about how he had tricked the Turks. He too was overjoyed to see Sarah, and he and Aaron finally told her about the decision to begin spying in earnest for the British. She also was stunned to learn that Alexander and Rivka were now in America. The three shared the frustrations they faced with the British and the perils of increasingly rapacious Turkish soldiers. Djamal's army had attempted yet another attack on Suez and been more soundly repulsed than the year before. The starving and badly demoralized common soldiers stumbled back through Palestine as an unruly mob taking revenge on Jewish villages along the way. The German officers who should have tried to restrain them instead clearly urged the Turks on to even more brutal reprisals.

This realization of an active German encouragement against the Jewish community brought a change in Aaron's early strategy of trying to win concessions and protection from Djamal Pasha, even as he sought to serve the British. Now there could be no going back. As Sarah recounted the horrors she had seen as she traveled and the deliberate extermination of the Armenians, Absalom ramped up his own militancy. Now it was not just a matter of escaping the Ottoman yoke. The real goal was the defeat of Germany and all the Central Powers. Only with a complete British victory, in the Middle East as well as on the Western Front, would *Eretz Israel* ever become a reality.

In the early weeks of 1916, Aaron was prodded further by an increased flow of intelligence coming from both Naaman Belkind and Josef Lishansky in the south. Something had to be done to reestablish contact with the British. Absalom once more insisted that he was the one to get to Lieutenant Woolley in Port Said. This time, instead of braving the perils of the desert, he would attempt the longer, and perhaps surer, route of leaving Turkey by way of the Balkans, specifically trying to reach Romania—which was still neutral—and then to Cyprus on his way to Egypt. Armed with letters from Aaron, he set out for Constantinople in March to win the necessary exit visas and travel permits.

Sarah was deputized to oversee the operations at Athlit while Aaron was away fighting a second season of locust infestations. He also continued courting Djamal in Damascus. What was intended as a temporary delegation by Aaron turned into an extended stay in the provincial capital when a horse-riding accident injured his leg and confined him to a bed in a hotel with a serious infection. Now it was up to Sarah to receive the agent reports and transfer them into the enciphered forms that would be loaded into waterproof leather bags in the event that the *Managem* ever stopped for a delivery.

Hardly had Absalom sent a telegram announcing that he had received permission to go to Romania than a miracle occurred at Athlit. Lieutenant Woolley had finally realized that the silence from the Athlit group could only be explained by their failure to get the new signal system information. He set out from Port Said in a small coastal schooner, pausing offshore near Athlit and putting a messenger ashore with a new set of instructions and encouragement to restart the flow of information from the network. Again, it was a close call. The messenger was a stranger to the neighborhood but managed to scramble up the slope to one of the garden beds. Then the dogs that Aaron had set out to warn of intruders began barking and the messenger was afraid to go farther to the house. In a panic he wedged the packet containing the letter and a set of new instructions from Woolley into the crossbar of a plow standing in the garden. Then he fled back to the rowboat just offshore and back to the schooner.

There was another stroke of luck. Aaron, still recovering, had managed to return from Damascus a few days earlier. The next morning as he walked through the garden beds near the station, he spotted the packet affixed to the plow before any of the Arab workers saw it. Aaron quickly dashed off a telegram to Absalom to abandon his journey through the Balkans and return to Zichron Ya'akov at once. Woolley's message put everything right. A new code and cipher system was included, along with an encouraging message that the navy chiefs in Port Said were eager for whatever intelligence they could provide. When Aaron had something to hand over, he was to hang dark-colored blankets from the station windows that faced the sea. The *Managem* would proceed up the coast on its blockade duties and then pause the next night for the transfers of Gideonite intelligence and new queries.

As so often happened in the Aaronsohn saga, fortune suddenly took a turn for the worse. They had no way of knowing that Lieutenant Woolley would never make it back to Port Said. As he continued up the coast to the port city of Alexandretta to contact naval intelligence sources, the small vessel was torpedoed by a Turkish cruiser and sunk. He was captured by the Turks and held prisoner for the rest of the war. No one in the Port Said headquarters bothered to restart the contacts.

Disturbing news came from Turkish newspapers a few weeks later. While Djamal Pasha's second offensive had failed in January, a reorganized force in April had trapped thirteen thousand British and Indian troops at Kutal Amara in the desert and forced them to surrender. With the survivors of the Gallipoli disaster still being ministered to, there now was no prospect that General Murray would undertake an attack across the Suez into Palestine.

During May and June, Aaron, Sarah, and Absalom fretted under the renewed isolation from their British contacts. Meanwhile, life among the Jewish settlements—indeed all of Syria–Palestine—grew more dire. The efforts to control the second locust infestation had met with slightly better results, but crops that were supposed to tide the population through the winter were clearly not sufficient, while the demands of Turkish authorities for greater contributions grew. Finally, Aaron made one of his typically bold decisions. Rather than try to reach the British in Cairo he would go to the source of ultimate authority, the British government in London.

This was a far riskier venture but to the three comrades it made sense. The Asquith government in London had been replaced by one led by the more dynamic, albeit erratic, David Lloyd George, and a coalition of forces that had pledged a far more vigorous prosecution of the war—both on the Western Front and in the Middle East. General Murray, it was rumored in the Turkish press, was on his way out, to be replaced by a commander that Lloyd George demanded "have more dash."

Moreover, Aaron was well aware that Chaim Weizmann, the leader of the powerful Zionist Movement in Europe, had great influence with the new Prime Minister and his senior ministers. Weizmann was a research chemist in Britain who used the name of Charles Weizmann on his many chemical patents. At the outbreak of the war, he donated to the government a formula for creating acetone, a crucial ingredient for the British war industries. Now he was the head of the government's commission on wartime research developments and had been instrumental in convincing Lloyd George that expanded efforts to knock the Turks out of the war were crucial. Later, of course, as Chaim Weizmann he would become the first president of the new state of Israel. But that was still to come; for the moment, Aaron counted on winning Weizmann's support for the Cairo command to make full use of the Gideonites.

Aaron was too large a figure (literally) to adopt the disguises that had enabled Alexander and Absalom to slip out of any Palestinian port city. His own prominence as a community leader and quasi-official of Djamal Pasha would mean his unexplained disappearance would soon be spotted and the reprisals against the occupants of Athlit and Zichron Ya'akov would be swift and horrible.

The scientific illiteracy of Turkish officials offered Aaron a way out. The Allied blockade and the unavoidable destructiveness of modern war meant the Turks were desperate for oil and lubricants of all kinds. Whether it was transport vehicles, artillery and machine guns, or ordinary rifles, the wear of battle and the pervasive corrosion of desert sand meant that the Turkish war machine needed oil. They had been reduced to trying to fabricate alternatives from the oils of the poisonous castor bean, but it was unsatisfactory as a substitute and insufficient in supply.

But, Aaron argued to Djamal, Syria–Palestine abounded in sesame, indeed sesame oil was already being pressed as a cooking additive. As an industrial lubricant it was useless, but the Turks could not know that and Djamal was desperate for a new source. Could Aaron devise such a conversion? Not at once, was Aaron's studied reply, but he knew of identical experiments at a prestigious Swedish institute where he had contacts. If he could just get permission to go there and confer with his Swedish colleagues and use their far more modern equipment, he was sure something would come of it.

In mid-July 1916, Djamal relented and Aaron set out for Constantinople with letters from the Pasha urging permits and authority to let him travel through the heart of the Central Powers and reach the neutral haven of Sweden. From there, passage to London would be easy. But once in Constantinople, Aaron found that Enver Pasha and his minions were intrigued but still suspicious. Instead of Sweden, Aaron was ordered to go to Berlin. Once there Aaron was to test his theories about sesame before his former mentors in the German scientific hierarchy. The German commanders advising Enver were determined to keep Aaron close since Germany too was starved of oils for food as well as lubricants.

Once in Berlin, Aaron duly underwent interviews with senior German scientists, including his old mentor Otto Warburg, who were initially skeptical since their own experiments with alternatives to petroleum-based fuels had been frustrating. But Aaron was at his best when he was arguing about science and he used his forceful personality as well as his scientific reputation to at least conditionally silence doubters. Besides, the Germans were well aware of the Swedish experiments and were not about to be caught lagging. After six weeks, in late August, Aaron was given permission to go to Sweden by way of neutral Copenhagen. He would be closely watched, he knew that. Also, both the Germans and Turks knew he had left family behind in Palestine; what better hostages to ensure he would return home if his theories proved correct?

Before he left Berlin, Aaron visited a woman friend from Palestine, a cousin of Naaman Belkind, who was studying there. She would serve as the conduit to get a message back to Absalom and Sarah, who were waiting impatiently at Athlit. Once he got to Copenhagen, Aaron used the delays in getting Swedish visas to enter that country to evade his German shadows and make his first contact with the British consul.

British officials are congenitally suspicious of strangers who show up offering intelligence schemes that seem too good to be true. So it was with Sir Robert Paget, the consul there, who politely declined to help Aaron get to Britain through any sub-terfuge about him going to America. But diplomats are civil servants and prudently he notified his superiors in the Foreign Office. To his surprise he got an instant response from an Admi-ral Reginald Hall, ordering him to find some clandestine way of getting Aaronsohn into the country without jeopardizing his cover as a Turkish citizen. "Blinker" Hall (so-called because one of his eyes twitched) was the head of a secret department known as NID, which was Britain's counterespionage service. Then Aaron produced a telegram from the U.S. Secretary of Agriculture (prompted by David Fairchild) stating that Aaron was an accredited consultant to the department and was urgently needed in Washington to help with food production.

Since the United States was still a neutral nation, Sir Robert and the London intelligence officials saw a way to get Aaron out of Copenhagen and into London without alerting the Germans or the Turks to his intentions. Passenger liners still sailed non-stop to America and were allowed to pass through the deadly blockades of both the Allies and Central Powers—even with the necessity of pausing at a coaling station in the remote Orkney Islands at the northernmost tip of Scotland to refuel for the long haul across the Atlantic. British officials routinely boarded such ships for inspections of passenger documents and cargo, since the Orkneys also included the huge port of Scapa Flow where the Royal Navy's High Seas Fleet was berthed. But since passengers had American visas or passports, the Germans did not object lest they further provoke the Wilson Administration.

There remained some problems. The only liner scheduled to embark from Copenhagen at the moment was a Scandinavian–American liner that was fully booked with the last remnants of American expatriates desperate to get home. But luck intervened. Two of the ticketed passengers were a pair of American rabbis who were returning after supervising a charity's supplies to relieve the starvation the Germans had wreaked on Belgium a year earlier. They knew of Aaron and agreed to let him share their cabin for the six-day trip from Denmark to Scotland. Meanwhile, Hall and his agency were busy with strategizing to get Aaron off the ship once it stopped at the coaling station at Kirkwall.

Finally on October 16, 1916, after nearly a month of delays, Aaron boarded the *Oskar II* and steamed away from Europe. Before he left, he sent a telegram to Naaman Belkind's cousin in Berlin to pass on to Sarah and Absalom at Athlit. There is uncertainty as to the exact language, or perhaps the telegram was garbled in transla-tion on its way. The message was clearly meant to be read by both German and Turkish intelligence, and on its surface it merely said that Aaron had grown frustrated sitting in Copenhagen trying to get a visa to enter Sweden. He had changed his mind and would go to neutral America instead. There, he added, his friends at the U.S. Department of Agriculture would certainly be more cooperative in his sesame experiments.

Instead of taking the hint that he was on his way to London at last, Sarah and Absalom were confused and alarmed. They wondered if Aaron had given up trying to win British support and had gone on to seek aid in America. Neither of them could suppress a fear that he had become disheartened with the cause they fought for and had joined Alexander and Rivka to sit out the war in safety and ease.

The confusion and fear that Aaron had abandoned them gripped both Sarah and Absalom at a vulnerable time. They spent hours of isolation in the upper room of the station keeping a constant watch for any sign that the British wanted to resume contact. Their conversations grew more personal and then dangerously intense. Sarah poured out her sorrow at the loveless marriage she had made. There was no question of a divorce. But there was no question either that she would ever go back to Constantinople. Before he had left Athlit the summer before, Aaron had written to Chaim to stop demanding her return or threatening to come retrieve her. In his turn, Absalom confessed that his proposal to Rivka had been a mistake. It was Sarah he had loved from the start and it was Sarah whom he loved still, now even more than ever. His only excuse was that the four-way relationship that linked him with Aaron, Sarah, and Rivka had confused him into thinking one was interchangeable with the other. He was wrong. Sarah was the only one he truly loved.

Sarah gave way to her isolation, her fatigue, her fear, and her own inner passion. Shy confessions of affection blended easily into professions of love. Tentative kisses and hugs became more intimate as the winter nights became longer and lonelier. Finally there came the caresses of love itself with its exhilaration and release. For a few weeks at the end of that year the two lovers enjoyed each other without shame or restraint. There were moments when the two even dreamed of a life together after the clouds of war had been blown away by liberation. Rivka and the rest of the family would understand, and they could live a long life of joy and promise in the new land they had helped to create.

The euphoria of new love, of course, could not last. The constant threats of discovery by the Turks and suspicion of their neighbors in Zichron Ya'akov grew frightening. A delegation of village elders had summoned Sarah to a meeting and demanded that whatever was going on at the Athlit station cease at once. Djamal Pasha had suddenly ordered the entire Jewish community of the city of Jaffa and its suburb of Tel Aviv to be expelled and their property seized under the pretext that there were saboteurs at work there. Other Jewish neighborhoods in the main port cities also were being brutalized and the refugees fled by the hundreds to any relatives they had in the more remote settler farm villages. Zichron Ya'akov was jammed with these destitute exiles; thousands more had been driven out to primitive camps in the desert, where famine and exposure were certain.

Did Sarah want such a catastrophe to be visited upon them, the elders demanded? If she did not promise to disband the spy group rumor said she was running, the elders told her they had no choice but to denounce her to Colonel Bek and his torturers. Sarah refused to admit what her spy band was doing but said, instead, she needed time to make changes in the workers at the station and perhaps then their suspicions would abate. Since the elders were not exactly certain what was going on, they grumbled but finally gave her time.

The flow of intelligence was creating a backlog of information that was time-sensitive. Yet how were the British to learn of it? Against her better judgement and against her own emotional intuition, she finally gave in to Absalom's own frustration at being idle. He would go again to Cairo and seek out Woolley and rebuild the contacts to allow the intelligence flow to finally help hasten British liberation.

While Sarah refused to admit her fears, Absalom's impatience got the better of him. He would not wait. So once again he would try to cross the Sinai to reach British outposts. This time his cousin Josef Lishansky, who had been the group's man on the southernmost border of Palestine, insisted on accompanying him. He had recently come to Athlit to play a more active role, but now argued that he knew the desert passes to British outposts better than Absalom. As he and Josef organized their journey, Absalom wrote a letter to Lieutenant Woolley in the belief that he was still in Port Said. If a ship did come after he left, it could warn Woolley of his arrival.

The letter said, "I have made up my mind, whatever may happen, that I shall try to cross the desert in order to reach you. . . .

"I have to run my last course, and I wish you to note that I am doing this in service to His Majesty George V, King of England, whom I have already crowned in my thoughts as King of *Eretz Israel* and Mesopotamia. . . . I wish you testify to this in order that it may be said to my comrades here, to those who tomorrow will be your comrades in arms. . . ."

After planning the route that seemed safest, and securing camels sturdy enough to endure the trek, the pair set out in mid-January of the New Year.

With his flair for the dramatic, Absalom had left Sarah a poem on the table of the station's room where they had found happiness:

If we shall fall before we reach our goal.
If we should not be privileged to see
Our people safe returned to the ancestral home
A nation proud and strong and free
Then to our sons and daughters we bequeath
Our places in the ranks of liberty.

CHAPTER SEVEN

Sarah Takes Command

•••••••••••••••••••••••

January–March 1917

Sarah, ca. spring 1917

As the war staggered into the new year of 1917, Sarah's sense of isolation brought the added strain of unexpected criticism about the spy band's activities from her neighbors and even from within her own family.

It was bad enough that Absalom and Josef Lishansky had disappeared into the desert, and the silence was ominous. There was no way of knowing their fate, and an added vexation was the fact that Alexander and Rivka had also vanished into a world of wealthy friends in New York. Another brother, Shmuel, had migrated to America before the war as well. The remaining brother, Zvi, became more active in the spy group's activities in the area around Zichron Ya'akov, but he also began to complain that he should take command and that Sarah should step aside. Absalom's cousin Naaman Belkind had come north to Athlit to work more directly, but he was young and prone to the same reckless enthusiasm as Absalom. Nor did he stay for long because he was needed at the winery at Rishon-le-Zion.

So Sarah relied upon herself. This transformation of Sarah Aaronsohn became complete, and she more than any of the men in her life truly became, as some later called her, the Flame of Israel. Aaron had gathered the first dozens of spies (mostly Gideonites), and Sarah now set out to recruit new sources of intelligence. The original Gideonite band had operated under the guise of fighting the locust infestations of the two past years in largely rural areas. Now Sarah singled out men and women whose occupations gave them special vantage points to report on specific Turkish regiments, the supply depots that supported them, and the state of the rapidly deteriorating network of railroads and bridges by which Djamal's army would maneuver if he mounted another attack on the British.

Accompanied only by the family's loyal Arab driver Abu Farid, Sarah took the carriage and went first to an important railroad junction at Afula, thirty miles east of Athlit. She sought out a Jewish physician, Dr. Moshe Neiman, who had been drafted into the Turkish Army as a medical officer. Neiman had started out as the pharmacist in the tiny clinic in Zichron Ya'akov many years earlier, and he had remained a friend of the Aaronsohn family.

He remembered Sarah as a young girl and was taken aback by the assertive woman who now tried to recruit him into the spy group. He at first tried to delay by saying he wanted to talk to Aaron, but Sarah asserted that she now was in charge of the spy group and she challenged him to take the same risks. It was his duty to inspect all new Turkish and German troops arriving to strengthen the battle lines around Beersheba. He also treated the wounded who were brought back. He had heard the Turks boast of the looting they had inflicted on the Jewish settlements and he had suffered the scorn of the German officers, so he cautiously agreed to pass on information of troop units, their condition, and the weapons and equipment moving through the rail junction to various sectors. After stopping at a coffee bar run by another agent, Sarah and Neiman moved on to Nazareth where the group had operatives who had unaccountably fallen silent. One of the agents had been caught lurking around an army supply depot and was so badly beaten that his wife forbade him to take further risks. Others had been alarmed at a large number of German soldiers who had recently been stationed there; they were more suspicious than the Turks and more likely to shoot suspects out of hand. Sarah managed to convince several agents to resume cautious reporting before she returned home.

To go farther away from Athlit was impossible. A woman traveling alone, and a Jewish woman at that, faced grave risks even with an Arab escort. Then, too, Athlit could not run itself without supervision, and suspicious neighbors in Zichron Ya'akov closely watched her coming and going. The pressure of time was building on Sarah as well. Aaron had been gone since July, when he set out for Constantinople. She had to believe that he had reached London by now and that quite possibly he had gotten to Cairo, where reunited with Absalom and Josef, they all would be busy hastening the day when the British would finally liberate Palestine from the Turkish yoke. When Aaron finally did return to Athlit she had to be ready with a trove of up-to-the-minute intelligence.

Aaron's usual abrupt temper was near to exploding in the first weeks after his arrival in Egypt in mid-December, 1916. He had arrived in an ill-concealed fury at the waste of time imposed upon him by chance and the stubborn plodding of various bureau-crats—Turkish, German, and, lastly, British. In July he had left for Constantinople, where he wasted nearly six weeks just getting his exit visas. It had taken more than a month after he journeyed to Berlin to convince German scientists and then officials that his theories on sesame oil as a source of both food additive and lubri-cant were worth pursuing. Then another month was wasted in Copenhagen until his clandestine escape could be set in motion.

Back in October while Sarah and Absalom were confined to their fruitless watch at Athlit, Aaron at last embarked on his six-day trip across the North Sea. He made himself conspicuous by appearing in the ship's public lounges and walking briskly on the outside decks taking vigorous exercise. As was his habit, he struck up acquaintances with many of the young women aboard; he was a manly figure of some celebrity and had a bachelor's taste for romantic flirtations. One attractive, more mature lady espe-cially caught his eye. Her name was Olga Bernhardt and she was traveling on an American passport. Once she learned that Aaron was a Turkish citizen, she confided she was a German by birth and archly hinted that she had many contacts in New York who were sympathetic to the Kaiser and Germany and its Turkish ally. It was clear to Aaron that if she was not officially a spy she surely could contact many of the German agents operating in America. She would be a credible witness to the scenario that would be played out in Kirkwall in a few days' time.

Finally, on October 16, the *Oskar II* anchored in Kirkwall, Scotland, and British military police boarded for a routine check of the passenger lists and their documents. When the inspectors came to Aaron, they abruptly took him below to the cabin where he had berthed and shortly afterward surprised the other passengers by escorting him and his luggage to the gangway. The liner's captain was informed that they had found Aaron's bags "full of German stuff" and that he was under arrest. As he was being led ashore, Olga Bernhardt tried to protest what was clearly a violation of American neutrality. She called after him that she would see that the American public was made aware of this arrest of an internationally famous scientist and consultant to the U.S. government. She was as good as her word, and the day she arrived in New York she gave a heated interview, which was prominently published in the *Evening Post* newspaper. The article was duly reported home by both the German and Turkish legations and Aaron's cover was preserved. That he was supposedly in custody in Britain was of small matter to both governments; Djamal Pasha may have regretted losing the agricultural expertise he had depended upon, but he was just as pleased to be rid of that vexing Jew who had demanded so much of him. The important point was that no suspicion had fallen on Sarah or the other spies.

What happened next to Aaron was the stuff of a boys' adventure novel. The British inspectors put him in the care of a kindly sergeant-major at the Kirkwall barracks, and a guard was assigned to accompany him to a nearby hotel for refreshment. He spent the night in the barracks guard house. In the morning two army officers accompanied him on an express train to London where he was taken at once to Scotland Yard. In a bit of comedy, the party arrived after most officials had gone home for the day, so Aaron was told to come back the next morning and turned loose to find a room for the night. London at that time was in a total blackout because of German zeppelin raids terrifying the city, so the darkened streets were largely empty as Aaron wandered about looking for a place to eat and then a hotel that had a room.

While Admiral Hall's counterespionage department had organized Aaron's defection into Britain, the overall Naval Intelligence hierarchy had to be convinced of his bona fides. After he arrived at Scotland Yard the next day he was subjected to a four-hour questioning by a Sir Basil Thompson, who doubled duty as head of the Yard's famed Criminal Investigation Division (CID) and since the war's start as deputy to the overall head of Naval Intelligence. It took five more days of idleness before Aaron was brought in for a second round of questioning. Even then he had no opportunity to display his trove of desert maps and data on the state of the Turkish Army.

Britain was in crisis that autumn of 1916. The debacle at Gallipoli the year before had been added to the gloom over the muddy stalemate in France. The other British ally, Tsarist Russia, was floundering on the brink of revolution. Public reaction at home to the institution of mandatory conscription was resentful, and the shaky coalition Asquith government was clearly sliding into a vote of no confidence in Parliament.

What this meant for war planners both in the Foreign Office civil service and on the British General Staff was that a top-to-bottom change in leadership and strategy was imminent. It behooved the bureaucracy to start the process of a new strategy before a new set of political leaders could preempt their power. One of the politicians whose opinions now became important for them to consider was the current Minister of War, the wily and dynamic David Lloyd George. Despite being in Asquith's cabinet, Lloyd George had been vocal in his criticism of the sluggish prosecution of the government's war efforts. He had vaulted to power in 1915, when the press and public were outraged to learn that the British artillery in France was running low on shells. As Minister of Munitions, he had dramatically boosted production and was promoted to the War Ministry in July 1916, where he made headlines by rejecting President Wilson's offer to mediate a brokered peace between the combatants, saying, "The fight must be to the finish."

Not only did this mean that when Lloyd George was asked to form a new government, as was likely, the field commanders in France would be pressed for a more aggressive strategy to break the bloody stalemate in the trenches. It also meant a new emphasis would be pressed for an all-out effort against the Turks, not in the north at the Dardanelles, but along the static Egyptian front stretching from Palestine into the far desert regions rimming that strategic artery along the Suez Canal. And indeed, in December 1916, two days after Lloyd George became Prime Minister in a coalition government of his Liberals and the Conservatives, he tasked British High Command with increased aggressiveness in France as well as with the capture of Jerusalem and an all-out offensive against the Turks in Palestine. "Jerusalem by Christmas" of the next year became the order of the day.

Lloyd George always had more than one reason for everything he did. While he was too much of a skeptic to be one of the evangelicals who saw the establishment of *Zion* as a prerequisite to the Second Coming of the Christian Messiah, he had developed a sympathy for a Jewish state in Palestine well before he reached power. As a young attorney in London, his firm had represented numerous clients who were Zionists, and with the start of the war Chaim Weizmann had become a close personal adviser on war production policies. He also shared with most of Britain's political elite at the time a dim view of the region's Arab leadership as a dependable partner in securing the Empire's access to the potential oil wealth of the region. Palestine's Jews, however, were another matter.

For once, fortune and coincidence tilted in Aaron's favor. The navy's spy masters suddenly were ordered to send Aaron to the Foreign Office where, to his surprise, he was greeted by Lord Eustace Percy, an old friend from his time in Washington when he visited the House of Truth boardinghouse headquarters of elite young American Progressives. Percy was about to become the chief foreign policy adviser to Arthur Balfour, who was made Foreign Secretary in the new Lloyd George government. Even more surprising, the principal foreign policy adviser to the new Prime Minister himself was to be another House of Truth alumnus, Philip Kerr.

Both friends could vouch for Aaron's credentials as a celebrated man of science; they also shared with the new government a commitment to a more aggressive military program in the Middle East in general and on the Palestine front in particular. Again Aaron's luck held, for on October 26, he was finally passed on to the War Office and directed to see a young army major named Walter Gribbon, who was in charge of its intelligence section for the Middle East. Gribbon was probably the only army officer in London at the time who knew just how deficient the state of knowledge was at General Murray's headquarters in Cairo. There were no accurate maps of Palestine in general or of the Gaza desert rimming the Turkish fortifications. The state of the Turkish Fourth Army was vastly overestimated. Gribbon had been an intelligence officer at the brigade level in the Mesopotamian sector and had been seriously injured in a raid to spy on the enemy fortifications. After being brought back to

England to recover, he was put in charge of this newly created section where there was very little dependable information to work with, and pressure was building from senior commanders for authoritative guidance.

Suddenly here was Aaron Aaronsohn, who could be vouched for by Weizmann as a distinguished scientist and who apparently had a stash of accurate maps and intelligence about the state of the Turkish Fourth Army. More tantalizing, he talked about how he had already organized a group of Jewish spies prepared to deliver even more up-to-date information about Turkish defenses and future plans for another Ottoman attack. Gribbon was a rarity on several counts. Anti-Semitism was only one of the entrenched bigotries of European and American cultures in those days and it was at its most virulent among the British officer class, which viewed Jews, along with Indians, Africans, and other ethnic groups within their empire as, at best, "wogs" (worthy Oriental gentlemen) or, as Rudyard Kipling warned, "the white man's burden."

Gribbon was comparatively free of anti-Jewish prejudice and was one of a growing number of headquarters strategy planners who had a dim view of the current wishful thinking that the Arab Revolt in the desert regions would blossom into an effective force against the Turks. But at General Murray's command center in Cairo, an Arab uprising was still supported as a case of having to make do with any available resources to protect the Suez Canal at all costs; ousting the Turks from Syria–Palestine was still a secondary issue.

One has a certain sympathy for Murray. In the past two years his troop strength had been siphoned off for the disaster at Gallipoli, and the capture of another thirteen thousand British and Indian troops at Kutal Amara had panicked him. The final months of 1916 had been devoted to occasional probes of Turkish positions in the desert to determine if another attack was coming. In the meantime, the British pushed construction of a railroad that ran alongside the canal so Murray could shift his forces more quickly. They also kept extending an elaborate water pipeline system from inside Egypt to the front. Despite a number of mechanized vehicles his army was still heavily dependent on horse-drawn transport and mounted cavalry; both horses and men could not hope to fight in the desert without a dependable supply of water.

What so excited Gribbon and other planners who saw Aaron's intelligence trove was that his hand-drawn maps clearly proved the British did not have to be tied to a water pipe supply if and when they attacked the heavily fortified enemy positions along the coastal road. Aaron showed them that the Bedouin for years had preserved a series of primitive wells that tapped into the plentiful water table that had made much of the region such a garden spot in Biblical times and that lay not too far beneath the surface. A British attack force need only take along fairly basic drills and pumps and cross the Gaza waste in safety. And that clearly meant a successful flanking attack could bypass the coast, capture the oasis city of Beersheba, and the Turkish front would by necessity collapse in on itself. Jerusalem by next Christmas was no longer just the new Prime Minister's fantasy.

With Aaron's help, Gribbon edited his notes of their conversations and the intelligence documents he had been handed and turned them into a thirty-one-page report that was then passed up the line to senior policymakers. The memorandum caused a stir that had fortunate consequences on another front. Aaron was sent to meet with one of the true historic forces in the entire postwar history of the Middle East—a deputy to Foreign Minister-to-be Arthur Balfour named Mark Sykes. Wily, devious, and something of an intellectual renegade, Sykes had traveled widely in the region and was the authority on what could and could not be done to wrest the huge province from Ottoman hands. One of the most closely held secrets in high government circles was that back in early May 1916, Sykes had brokered with French diplomat François Georges-Picot the infamous Sykes–Picot agreement that portioned out shares of Syria–Palestine and its mineral riches between the two powers. The pact blithely ignored the promises of a postwar Arab national state made by British emissaries from the Cairo military headquarters to the leaders of the various tribal factions.

Sykes was both a devout Roman Catholic and a typical upper-class anti-Semite who thought of Jews only as a distasteful presence in the seedy world of international finance. This new arrival named Aaron Aaronsohn was something else, however, and Sykes had the wit to recognize it. After a brief meeting at the Foreign Ministry, Sykes invited him to dinner for what turned into a series of conversations that changed his attitude, not to Jews generally but to the prospect that a loyal Jewish community in Syria–Palestine (under a British mandate, of course) might prove crucial to imperial control of its share of the land once the war was won. Not only would a Jewish state of the kind advocated by Aaron be a more plausible alternative to one controlled by Arabs, Sykes also realized it would draw the international support of leading Zionists in Europe and America and be an effective buffer against any French encroachment. This change in attitude on his part had an important impact on two counts that Aaron could only guess at. The inevitable slow pace of the bureaucratic process at the War Office was speeded up by Sykes's interest, and the Gribbon-edited report was sent at once to General Murray's planners in Cairo, where it created an approving stir.

Not so fortunately, Aaron's improved status brought him into contact and conflict with Chaim Weizmann, now both an intimate adviser to the Prime Minister and also the London head of the World Zionist Organization. Based in neutral Denmark, the WZO had steadfastly insisted on protecting its postwar status by refusing to side with either the Central Powers or the Allies. Weizmann walked a delicate line then. He was an important adviser in Britain's war production efforts and yet he would not be seen publicly as taking sides. He knew that Aaronsohn had very important critics back in Palestine among the WZO leaders there, particularly on matters of getting and distributing the vital financial aid from America necessary to keep the impoverished settlements alive. And now, in their meetings in London, Weizmann was angered when Aaron not only insisted on continuing to solicit money from American Zionists but also demanded the WZO provide him with funds to support his spying operations. The idea of being caught funding spies inside Palestine outraged nearly all of the Zionist officials and led to a long-running and vexing dispute between the two men that would last beyond the war. Nor, it must be said, was Weizmann happy to see Aaron elevated to any importance as a Jewish spokesman in British eyes, and Aaron's brusque manner annoyed him. His annoyance increased considerably in 1917 when he was called as an adviser to help in the drafting of Foreign Secretary Arthur Balfour's famed declaration of Britain's pledge for a Jewish homeland in Palestine, and found Sykes citing Aaron's advice on specific boundaries.

For the moment, however, Aaron had other problems. For one thing, he was broke. His War Office hosts had begun to pay his hotel bills and other expenses but he wanted to take a sizable sum of financial aid with him to Cairo to send on to Athlit for community aid and for the spy operations. This, Gribbon's superiors argued, was money best paid out by General Murray's paymasters, who could keep a more prudent eye on its use. Aaron predictably was insulted. He was even more frustrated when his letters to American Zionists begging for funds to take with him drew a delayed response and then, at the last minute, a wire for a paltry $500 arrived. As a final frustration, he had wanted Alexander to come at once to London to continue lobbying in his behalf before coming to Cairo to help him. Although Alexander agreed readily enough, it soon became evident that when he did come, Aaron might be gone from London.

Other bureaucratic delays sorely tested Aaron's temper. There were arguments over whether the Cairo headquarters staff was to take command of operations and send officers to take control. Aaron managed to quash that idea, but it was still never decided just what role he was to play in the army's planning for a Palestine campaign—if in fact there was one finally set in motion. And at the last moment, Royal Navy forces within the War Office argued that since they had first supported the early operations when the army would not, their intelligence officers in Port Said should be Aaron's first destination before he was handed on to Cairo. This, reluctantly, Aaron agreed to. Finally, Major Gribbon was able to secure a formal letter to a General Gilbert Clayton, who was the senior intelligence officer at Murray's General Headquarters staff in Cairo, stating that Aaronsohn was to be used both as a director of his band's operations and as an important adviser for the Palestine campaign that London now demanded.

So, on November 24, 1916, Aaron boarded the P&O passenger liner *Karmala* bound for Port Said. On a slow and zigzag route designed to avoid German submarine patrols, Aaron continued his regimen of pacing around the ship and pouring his frustrations into his diary. When the ship finally docked in Port Said on December 12, Aaron found to his surprise that his Royal Navy handlers showed none of the enthusiasm for his arrival that he had been promised in London. He was put in the charge of a navy captain, William Stanley Edmonds, who forbade Aaron to leave for Cairo to see the army and then offered him the meager stipend of £1 a day, which would not cover a hotel room.

Contrary to his instructions from Gribbon in London to work with the army, he was baffled to be told by Captain Edmonds that the navy insisted on a prior claim. It was the navy that had first vetted him in London, and then claimed jurisdiction over him because of the previous contacts between Absalom Feinberg and the now-imprisoned Lieutenant Woolley. Not that the navy admitted to any commitments, since Woolley had not written down any.

Edmonds made no effort to conceal his irritation at having to waste time on this stranger, a Jew no less, and his suspicious claims of a spy operation already up and running in Palestine. Aaron was made to understand that Edmonds's commanding officers were constantly being warned that foreign spies were being sent over by the Turks and Germans to mislead them.

After much fierce argument, the navy grudgingly provided Aaron with a small underpowered schooner to try to reach Athlit and reestablish contact with Sarah and Absalom. He was, however, strictly forbidden to go ashore himself. Through contacts with the same Palestinian Jewish émigrés who had befriended Absalom on his earlier quest, a volunteer was recruited to make the trip by skiff from the schooner and then swim three hundred yards to the agricultural station with a leather bag of gold coins and new orders, and to return with whatever new intelligence Sarah might have collected.

As in the past, the attempts could be made only on nights when there was no moonlight. There were, in fact, two such voyages; both ended with Aaron in a rage of frustration. On one trip the recalcitrant ship's captain refused to get near enough to see whether anyone at the station was signaling that the coast was clear. On the second, undertaken in the last week of January, the sea was so stormy that the messengers were put ashore but had to be abandoned at Athlit with no return of information about the state of conditions there.

The attempted landings from the trawler had been a meager gesture that Edmonds was reluctant to repeat. Worse, he refused Aaron's requests for adequate funds to set up his own operations, leaving him having to solicit support from Palestinian émigrés in the Alexandria Jewish enclave. As a final insult, Edmonds suggested that he might be willing to send one of his own agents to take over the operation at Athlit, and the two men ended up shouting at each other.

If Sarah was unaware of the delays in reaching her, Aaron had no idea of the peril that surrounded his sister. He assumed that Absalom and Josef were both carrying most of the burden of overseeing the spy group. He decided to bluff his navy handlers and threatened that if he could not go to the army in Cairo, he would return to London and appeal directly to his War Office handlers. Edmonds, in a mix of fear and irritation, told him to go.

CHAPTER EIGHT

Sarah Gets Her Orders and NILI Gets Its Name

• •

January–March 1917

On January 4, 1917, Aaron borrowed some money from his friends and traveled to Cairo, taking a room in the Continental Hotel, where he had stayed on earlier visits for scientific conferences before the war. The hotel now also housed most of the officers attached to various army intelligence services, including staff members attached to the year-old think tank known as the Arab Bureau.

The Arab Bureau had been a hastily organized collection of scholars, archaeologists, and explorers—selected by the Ashmolean Museum's director D.G. Hogarth—who had any knowledge of the Middle East in general and the Egyptian–Palestine war front in particular. The group had two important tasks that were desperately needed by General Murray's planners. First, it was to produce a series of briefing booklets for force commanders to use in operations in specific sectors of the vast uncharted regions of the Arabian theater. Second, the staff was to work to win the support and cooperation of the widely diverse Arab tribes in what would, after the war, be organized into a protectorate under British control and exploitation. In neither of those two objectives was there any consideration of Palestine or of a Jewish state within that protectorate, despite what the government in London was hinting to Zionist leaders.

Stewart Newcombe had been made a senior officer of the bureau, largely because he, young T.E. Lawrence, and Leonard Woolley had in 1913 conducted a preliminary and not very accurate survey of the Gaza and Sinai desert areas that might be used by the Turks in any attacks on the Canal. Hogarth, who was the mentor of so many of them, was given a navy captain's rank and divided his time as a referee for the inevitable quarrels within the staff and advising General Clayton of intelligence and General Murray.

At first the only bureau person who would talk to Aaron was one of the mythic figures in the histories of British Middle East involvement—Gertrude Bell, later known as the Desert Queen. Bell was a sister in spirit to Sarah in so many ways. At seventeen, she had been one of the first women to earn an honors degree in history at Oxford and had gone on to set records as an Alpine mountain climber. In 1900 she had begun a series of journeys throughout most of Syria–Palestine, moving ever deeper into the still uncharted deserts of Mesopotamia searching for the abandoned traces of once-famous Biblical cities. In addition to mastering French, German, and Italian, she became fluent in Turkish and most of the Arab dialects.

There was a physical and emotional resemblance between the two women. Gertrude had bright red hair and piercing blue eyes and an athletic build made fit by her skills as an outdoors enthusiast and fearless horsewoman. She too had the open heart for romantic love, but like Sarah, her choice did not lead to marriage. Her one documented romance was with a married British diplomat and soldier and when he died at Gallipoli, she never gave her heart to another.

When Hogarth had arrived in Cairo as an adviser to the British High Command, he had sent for Bell especially because she, more than any of the other so-called Arabists, had the most thorough knowledge of the unexplored territories, their geography, and various peoples. Before the war, she had published a number of popular books of photographs and histories of the various sites she had visited that fueled a wide public interest in what was popularly known as the Holy Land. As early as 1909, she had begun excavations at the enormous site of the Hittite city of Carchemish, the same place that later would attract Woolley and Lawrence. She also had formed remarkable friendships with a wide number of Arab chiefs, including those of the notorious brigand tribe known as the Howeitat. She viewed Lawrence as a young, talented, but not altogether trustworthy junior colleague. She dismissed his fascination with the desert tribes led by Sharif Hussein and his son Prince Faisal as being a waste of time and money that could be better spent on her Hashemite favorites.

Aaron, however, was someone whose encyclopedic knowledge of the geology, the flora, and the people of the entire Syrian–Palestinian region exceeded her own. And perhaps this six-foot-tall, enormous young man with his dynamic personality had a measure of attractiveness for her as well. She by now was nearly forty-nine, and the forty-one-year-old Aaron was closer to her age than the younger bureau scholars. But like Sarah, Gertrude Bell had the habit of setting her emotions aside in order to draw greater satisfaction from going her own way and choosing her friends—and foes. Her lifelong crusade was to win nationhood for her chosen people, who after the war would form the new nation of Iraq.

Bell was intrigued by Aaron's argument that General Murray could hasten his attack to capture Jerusalem by skillful exploitation of Aaron's careful maps of the secret desert wells guarded by the Bedouin, and by using easily obtainable water well drills and pumps to punch no deeper than three hundred feet to tap into long-forgotten aquifer reservoirs that had made many of the old Biblical towns gardens of plenty. Sensing his isolation, she took him to Groppi's, a restaurant that featured ice cream and various coffees and was a favorite of the Arab Bureau staff. But there was not much else she could offer, given the structure of the Arab Bureau's hierarchy.

She did at least direct Aaron to two newly arrived officials who could get him the audience he sought with Generals Clayton and Murray. William Ormsby-Gore and Wyndham Deedes turned out to have read Aaron's London memorandum and were intrigued by the prospects. They had been sent to Cairo as part of the Lloyd George government's determination to spur the pace of attacks on the Turks. They both questioned Aaron closely and offered support but, as usual, advised patience. Things were changing—but change took time. Aaron was advised to go back to Alexandria and try to secure a second attempt by the navy to reach Athlit and return this time with more immediate intelligence.

For once, Aaron did not protest. But before he could set out for Alexandria he was surprised to suddenly be confronted by a solemn Captain Edmonds, who had come to Cairo to find him. Aaron was abruptly informed that one of his band of spies had turned up badly wounded at an Australian outpost on the battle line. He rushed to a field hospital in Port Said where he was horrified to find Josef Lishansky.

Lishansky had been found just outside the lines with three bullet wounds in his back and arm. The despondent Lishansky told Aaron that, despite Sarah's protests, he and Absalom had set out with a Bedouin guide to make a desert crossing to reach the British. As they were near success their guide abandoned them and may have betrayed them to other Bedouin who set out to capture them and turn them in to the Turks for a reward. In the ensuing gunfight, the two managed to get away but Absalom was mortally wounded and soon died, leaving Lishansky to stagger on alone.

Aaron was shattered. Absalom had become more like a brother than even his own kin. His death left a hole in his heart that never could be filled. And then, to add to his misery, was the sudden fear of what was happening to Sarah, now all alone at Athlit.

Aaron returned on the train to Cairo in a state of shock. When he confronted Edmonds and Deedes at the Arab Bureau offices, he collapsed in tears that soon turned to a rage and accused Edmonds of being "morally responsible for our misfortunes." While Edmonds probably felt no guilt for Absalom's death, he did manage to organize another attempt to reach Athlit two days later.

Again, the attempt was only partly successful. But now Aaron was being pressed for more current information by the new arrivals on the intelligence staff at headquarters. Deedes had asked for specific information about the state of Turkish fortifications on the coastline as far north as Haifa and the latest estimates of troop strength.

Aaron used his new friends to free himself from Alexandria and the control of Captain Edmonds. Deedes had assigned him office space in the Arab Bureau's quarters in the posh Savoy Hotel, and there in the last week of January he first met a diminutive, sloppily dressed lieutenant who affected the Arab *keffiyeh* headdress. In his diary Aaron tersely recorded meeting a "lieutenant Laurens" and noted that he was "very well informed on Palestine questions—but very conceited." Later, after Lawrence had begun to lecture Aaron with what the latter realized was a very superficial experience in the region, he amended his opinion further. Lawrence was, he judged, "a little snot."

What Lawrence thought of Aaronsohn is not recorded, but he probably paid scant attention to this enormous Jew who towered over him and seemed so sure of himself. Lawrence had other things on his mind. He was riding a wave of sudden celebrity that was as intoxicating as it was unexpected. For the past two months he had traveled throughout the desert regions meeting with Sharif Hussein and Prince Faisal, surveying what they needed of arms, equipment, and vast sums of gold, to turn the scattered tribal bands into a united military force to drive the Turks out of their positions threatening the Canal. Lawrence was only one of a number of more senior British Army officers who were working with the Arabs, and he had been sent out there by the Arab Bureau to get information and not to actually take a hand in organizing.

Yet when he was called back to Cairo to resume his desk-bound chores of drafting analysis memos, Prince Faisal surprised everyone by formally requesting Lawrence be assigned to him as an adviser. The High Command had little choice but to send him back after only a few days of conferences, but they sent him back with little hope of any dramatic results. The British hopes in the much publicized Arab Revolt had begun to wane already. As a fighting force the Arabs were effective enough in guerrilla raids on laxly fortified Turkish outposts and isolated railway lines. But they proved to be terrified of Turkish artillery and machine guns, and it soon was confirmed that some tribal leaders who were getting huge sums of British gold were also taking bribes from Djamal Pasha to leave certain strategic positions alone. None of this concerned Aaron, who had developed a disdain for Arab dependability, and was more committed than ever before to the goal of a Jewish state in Palestine—which did not include Arabs as political equals. More pressing for him was what to do about the tragedy of Absalom's death.

Aside from his deep personal grief at losing Absalom, who was closer to him than even his brother Alexander, there was a sudden horror at the thought of what would happen if the Turks should find Absalom's body. If he was recognized, Turkish security officers might connect Absalom's attempt to reach British lines as confirmation of rumors they were checking that there was a spy ring among the Jews. He feared Athlit's stores of intelligence might be discovered. If that happened, Zichron Ya'akov would surely suffer reprisals. There was another vexation: Jewish religious rules held that a person could not be considered dead if a body could not be found. How would the Feinberg family react if they were told of Absalom's death without being able to properly bury their relative?

For the moment secrecy was essential. Aaron managed to get Josef moved to a hospital in Cairo and made him promise to say nothing about the death. For those of Absalom's friends in the Jewish communities of Alexandria and Cairo, Aaron promoted a story that Absalom had been sent to Britain for flight training so he could take part in aerial reconnaissance with the Royal Flying Corps. It was a thin story but it would have to do.

Lishansky quickly recovered and joined Aaron at his office in the Savoy. Deedes, Ormsby-Gore; and other intelligence staff were impressed by his answers to the questions they had about the Turkish Army locations and strengths as well as the documents he had carried that pinpointed the most important fortifications.

The recognition of the importance of the information Sarah and her spies could supply was now apparent. This was a crucial time for the British. In January an ANZAC force of mounted infantry had pushed the Turks out of a substantial part of the Sinai Peninsula. Murray's upbeat report on the ANZAC action merely heated up London's demand for more dramatic action. While the Arab Bureau continued to churn out its operational manuals and analyses, the Army established its own Eastern Mediterranean Special Intelligence Bureau (EMSIB) to plan the broad attack demanded by London. General Clayton was in charge and Aaron's two new friends were part of the senior staff.

By mid-February, EMSIB had formally recognized the Athlit operation as an asset and assigned it the code name "A Organization." At the same time the steamer *Managem,* used by Woolley in the first attempts, again was reassigned to make contact with Sarah and Athlit. It was larger and better powered than the previous craft provided Aaron, and he hoped the next approach would be able to wait offshore to receive current intelligence—whatever the weather might be. It was now vital that Sarah and Athlit provide more current information since a formal campaign—later known as the First Battle of Gaza—was to be launched in early April.

By the start of 1917, Sarah was solely responsible for encouraging and collecting the growing flow of intelligence coming in from the three dozen active agents—Gideonites and ordinary citizens—whom she had recruited. But to what end? None of it had reached the British who were supposed to be the liberators. The sudden solitude marked the final turning point in Sarah's life.

Her father Ephraim had at first been kept in ignorance of what she was doing and, still grieving for the loss of his wife, he showed no interest. But finally she had made him aware and took comfort that while he remained on the sidelines, he seemed to approve. At least at first. Zvi began to complain to Ephraim that he should take charge at Athlit, that Sarah was causing alarm among the elders of Zichron Ya'akov with her sudden unescorted trips away to who-knew-where. And whenever Naaman Belkind arrived with fresh intelligence from the south, he had begun asking pointed questions about Absalom and his absence.

Her only reliable companion was something of a surprise. A local youth named Liova Schneersohn had accompanied Aaron to Constantinople the summer before, posing as his secretary. His real function was to stay there after Aaron set out for London and Cairo, and serve as a communications link so that messages sent through contacts in Berlin could be passed on to Sarah and Absalom. But by the end of 1916, Schneersohn had despaired of hearing any more from Aaron. Short of funds, and after warnings that Turkish authorities were suspicious of his identity papers, he returned to Haifa as the servant of a German officer. From there he ran away to Athlit and turned up at Sarah's door in early February.

Sarah welcomed Liova at first. He knew the area and knew how to arrange to meet other spy ring members without running afoul of Turkish police or nosy neighbors. Most of the time, however, he kept watch from Aaron's studio on the top floor of the station for signs that the British were trying to contact them from the sea. One problem developed. Liova soon fell in love with Sarah and, despite her discouraging him, he remained devoted to her. It was an inconvenient complication for Sarah, whose emotions already were under enough of a strain from worrying over the whereabouts of her brother and the fate of Absalom, the love of her life.

She had a brief respite of happiness when Aaron's second attempt to reach Athlit was successful. The navy had only provided Aaron with a small fishing trawler and while two young swimmers recruited from the Palestinian refugee community made it ashore, the captain of the vessel panicked at the rough seas and refused to wait for their return.

Sarah at first was delighted at the arrival of the young messengers, for they brought along with gold and fresh orders a personal gift: Aaron's magnifying glass and his penknife as a sign that he was back and in contact. But then she faced being stuck with the two boys, and her worries returned when they said they had never heard of Absalom having reached Egypt. The two strangers were a temporary problem to be kept from sight during the day until it could be arranged to safely spirit them away at night back to their home villages and their families. The money, a few hundred pounds, was an enormous relief—it meant she could pay the back wages of the loyal Arab workers at the station and replenish the scant supplies of food available for Ephraim at home. But most important was the proof that Aaron was back. She would carry on.

On the next attempt in early March, the *Managem* paused off Athlit during daylight, and after exchanging signals went on its patrol up the coast before returning under cover of darkness. Along with Aaron, a recovered Josef Lishansky was aboard—and it was he who was rowed ashore and greeted by Liova Schneersohn and another veteran, Gideonite Reuven Schwartz. Aaron had insisted on being in the skiff that beached and after an emotional reunion, Liova joined him to return to the ship.

Once aboard, Schneersohn almost at once asked about Absalom, and Aaron broke the tragic news to him. While the two comrades were mourning, one of the ship's officers approached them to ask what code signal password for the Athlit group should be used for future visits. Liova had included a pocket-sized Hebrew Bible that had been a gift from Absalom in his possessions and he turned to it. It was a custom to let the Bible fall open to a random page and to seek a sign from some line of Scripture. The book fell open to the Book of Samuel and counting down seven lines on the page they read the passage where Samuel, the high priest, rebukes King Saul, saying *"Nitzach Israel lo Ishakari,"* or, "The Eternity of Israel shall not lie." Taking the Hebrew initials, the two chose NILI as the group's name, and while the British continued to refer to it as "the A Organization," the NILI name quickly spread among the spy band as a brave call to arms.

Meanwhile at Athlit, Lishansky broke the terrible news of Absalom's death to Sarah. Lishansky's bags of British gold coins and supplies were vitally needed, but they were overshadowed by the loss of one of the group's mythic figure. Sarah must have been shattered by the rush of encouragement and horror that Josef brought. In tears he told her the details of his trek across the desert with Absalom. He told how the guide had deserted them, about the Bedouin ambush and running gunfight that had followed. He sobbed as he told how he struggled to drag Absalom's body away despite his own wounds, and how his friend had died in his arms. Through it all, Sarah remained stoic as if frozen. At the end, she told Josef that above all, he should not blame himself, then she sent him downstairs to rest and locked the door of her upper room to grieve alone.

Afterward, Sarah rarely spoke to anyone about her sorrow over Absalom's death. But in the next exchange of intelligence sent when the *Managem* returned, Sarah included two letters, one with intelligence written before Josef had come ashore, the other a reflection on the heartbreaking news. The second letter showed just how iron-willed she had become.

She wrote, "Enclosed here you will find the letter I wrote when I still knew nothing. Today I already know about our horrible disaster. But it is with a brave heart, filled with feelings of revenge that I want to continue his work. The disaster is too overwhelming to make comfort. But with courage God will let us live so that we may carry on. Nobody else here knows. . . ."

In the next exchange she told Aaron, "It is hard for me to put down on paper what I feel. . . . It is terrible and there is no comfort. But I must tell you that I am stronger than iron and very cool. I would never have believed that I could find such strength in myself. There are times when I feel as though I am dead or a worthless vessel, for how is it possible that I am able to restrain myself in the face of such an awful sacrifice? Maybe it is the work allotted to me, the debt I owe to continue the work our dear one began. Yes, I want only to continue. And revenge."

Later, in July, she was able to write a consoling letter to Rivka, still in New York. "Even if we succeed in our work and the redemption of Israel will have been achieved by such a sacrifice, I would not wish for such a sacrifice. However much we talk and however many tears we shed our hearts will not be lightened. . . . But why should I pour salt on the wound. You, Rivka, are miserable and suffering more than any of us. . . ."

One thing that emerged from the tragedy: Sarah resolved that she alone would remain in command of an organization she had expanded on her own. Whatever Aaron had intended, and whatever arguments Josef made, to hand over the reins of the group would be a betrayal of the memory of the man she had allowed herself to love. If tragedy had left her alone, so be it. She would carry on.

CHAPTER NINE

Sarah and NILI Make a Difference

•◆•◆•◆•◆•◆•◆•◆•◆•◆•◆•◆•

April–July 1917

Sarah and Josef Lishansky, Cairo, May 1917

In early March, the British High Command finally recognized the "A Organization" as its primary source of reliable intelligence from Syria–Palestine. The *Managem* began to make regular voyages to Athlit, bringing questions for specific information along with supplies, and, most important, twenty-pound leather sacks of British gold sovereign coins. The money was doubly important, for it meant Sarah could pay her Arab workers their back wages and Josef Lishansky could distribute tangible aid to the nearly destitute Jewish villages along the length of the coast.

Now time suddenly became important for the Cairo planners for up-to-the-minute intelligence. There were discussions about an attempt to send radio telegraphy equipment to Athlit, but it was rightly judged that it was too far for the broadcast technology of the time to make it possible. Instead, Sarah was surprised and a bit amused to have one of the early deliveries of supplies from the *Managem* bring crates of homing pigeons and instructions for their care and use for putting enciphered messages into tiny capsules that were fixed to one of the bird's legs.

Raising and training homing pigeons has for centuries been a popular hobby for breeders who raced them both in Europe and the Middle East. With a unique navigational skill, the birds can find their way home over distances of up to a thousand miles. Early warriors including Genghis Khan used them and the British Army had a special corps devoted to their training and use. Sarah received an official pamphlet that detailed how to construct the coops to house the creatures. Since the distance between Athlit and the EMSIB offices in Port Said was just under three hundred miles, NILI could now get critical news of troop movements there and on to Cairo in a day instead of two weeks.

The British also allowed Aaron to include money that had begun to come to him from his American Zionist supporters, who were unaware of his spying activities. While the new flow of funds did alleviate the near-starvation conditions in Palestine, it totaled a pittance when compared to the hundreds of thousands of pounds the British were investing to ignite the still-smoldering Arab Revolt.

There had been a problem immediately after Aaron's first successful landing at the station. Lishansky stayed behind and assumed that he would take command of the spy group, and at first was offended when Sarah flatly refused to hand over authority to him. He finally was convinced to follow her orders and was mollified when his role became more public as the dispenser of aid, while Sarah remained at Athlit logging in the intelligence information that arrived and organizing it for translation once it reached Cairo.

First, however, toward the end of March, the two set out on a marathon journey through the entire region. With their loyal Arab driver Abu Farid and the Aaronsohn family's sturdy carriage, they first traveled north to Damascus and took a room in the most prominent hotel there, which was the gathering place for off-duty German officers. Josef posed as a businessman and spent time in the bar while Sarah, more decorously, would take tea in the lobby or pretend to be writing letters. Since both were fluent in German it was easy enough to strike up conversations and overhear gossip.

Eight days later they arrived in Jerusalem, and found the modern Hotel Fast to be the favorite of young German officers on leave from the front. They repeated their earlier tactic and in two days gathered priceless details enabling them to produce a report estimating, among other details, that the Germans had roughly 50,000 troops throughout Syria–Palestine, along with their locations. They also acquired a map of the fortifications around Jerusalem, locations of artillery and machine guns as well as gossip about troop movements, changes in commanders, and the almost universal complaints about the corruption and incompetence of the Turks of the Fourth Army.

As they traveled between Damascus and Jerusalem they noted new bridges, the state of roads, and the various depots where the

Turks stored ammunition and fodder for their draft animals. Along the way they assigned new tasks to those NILI members who would be active providers of information and recruited more casual sources who were to support the active spies. The most important news was about Turkish plans to reinforce their positions along the Gaza, which ran from that city to its flank at Beersheba. This was vital intelligence since General Murray planned a major attack on those very positions in the first weeks of April.

One unexpected problem cropped up. While they were in the south they stopped at Rishon-le-Zion, where Naaman Belkind had assumed control of the NILI agents. When he came to a rendezvous with Sarah he was upset to find Lishansky with her and acting as an equal. He demanded to know what had happened to his cousin Absalom Feinberg, and dismissed their story of his going to England for flight training. He told Sarah privately that he suspected Lishansky had somehow betrayed Absalom, and was only temporarily mollified by her assurances.

The twelve-day journey was an exhausting ordeal, for even in the comfort of a carriage the main road was so rutted and ruined by the Turkish transports, and outside the main cities the accommodations were so primitive, that the malnourished Sarah got little rest. While the trip had been an intelligence success, it proved a public relations mistake. All the suspicious villagers of Zichron Ya'akov saw was Sarah and Josef in their stylish clothes arriving at the house on Founders Street after what appeared to be a scandalous holiday. Both Sarah and Josef were married to others, after all, so the envious drew their own conclusions and gossip flowed.

Oblivious to the suspicions of their neighbors, Sarah and Josef hastened to organize their up-to-date intelligence into reports in time for the next contact. Back at the Athlit station, they drafted a summary of all they had seen and heard. Then they combed through the trove of information that had arrived recently from other operatives.

The resulting file was enormous in bulk and the most current portrait of the state of the Fourth Army that could be obtained. Indeed, it was probably a better grasp of what the Turkish Army in the region was capable of than Djamal Pasha could have obtained from his own sources. When it arrived in Cairo ten days later, General Clayton's staff was able to circulate what in military parlance is called an order of battle.

Crediting "our most trusted source in Palestine," the document reported the precise number of troops in Djamal's army, but perhaps more importantly, it gave a realistic appraisal of the number of "effectives," soldiers who were actually fit enough and properly armed to be brought into action. The NILI reports, astonishingly, gave a precise listing of all the artillery, machine guns, airplanes, motorized transports, and rifles—which were in such short supply that many units had two infantrymen share a single weapon.

Aaron, in some of his early questions that he sent ashore to Sarah, admonished her to strictly report without comment or opinion on what the group was observing. He also chided her to require that the NILI operatives include in their reports more information about agricultural developments, reports on crops, rainfall, and other phenomena. Later he softened his instructions when the British intelligence analysts praised Sarah's reports that included German officer gossip and signs of rising public opposition to the orgy of public hangings that Djamal ordered to suppress dissent. There was even laughter when she reported that Djamal had ordered a new design of helmet worn by Fourth Army infantrymen and then patented it and lobbied the two other Pashas to make it standard issue throughout the Turkish Army. This example of Djamal's greed was considered excessive even by Turkish standards and caused a public opinion backlash that rippled all the way back to Constantinople.

The NILI spies also caused excitement among the senior British commanders with the first news that the Germans had begun to weaken their presence in Palestine. For much of the war the Kaiser had sent important senior commanders to provide the organizational skills and strategic planning the Turks had lacked. Equally important, German troops had bolstered key fortified points.

But now NILI reported that some of the better known German generals and whole units of line troops were being transferred back to the Western Front in France. This new information was a double insight of the highest importance. It meant the German resources were so stretched in France that forces were being brought back from elsewhere to boost the strength of the next huge offensive expected that spring. The Allies fully anticipated that as the Americans edged ever closer to joining the war, the Germans would attempt an all-out attack on the Western Front designed to force a victorious settlement before the tide could turn.

Equally cheering, a drawdown of German forces in Palestine also could reflect a growing doubt among planners in Berlin that their Turkish ally could ever seize the Suez Canal or force the British out of Egypt. If so, the time was quickly coming when a British attack might actually overrun Turkish positions and make the politically important capture of Jerusalem possible.

Harried by demands from London, General Murray had carefully reorganized his forces into a new formation that coupled foot infantry, mounted troops, and airplanes, called the Egyptian

Expeditionary Force (EEF). In planning his attack he selectively picked those NILI intelligence items arriving from Athlit that showed the weaknesses of the Fourth Army, and ignored the insights that argued for attacking the Turkish flank positions. As always, Murray was unwilling to try a flank attack on Beersheba because it was firmly believed that a large enough force could not be moved over the desert approaches where there was no water, despite Aaron's continued insistence that he had mapped the closely guarded wells of the Bedouin.

Instead, on March 26, a combined force of four divisions of British and ANZAC troops hit the Turks at their strongest point—the ancient coastal city of Gaza. The ground forces were bolstered by more than a dozen Royal Flying Corps planes dropping bombs on the city and on Turk gun emplacements. Even though the EEF managed to seize control of outer suburbs of Gaza, Murray's field commanders fretted over the approach of darkness and reports of Turkish reinforcements, and withdrew back to their old lines.

On April 17–19, the Second Battle of Gaza was fought. Again, Murray hurled the EEF against the strongest points of the Fourth Army positions. This time, however, despite early gains by the assault, the Turks had used the respite to add more artillery and machine guns. The air war also tilted their way with the arrival of half a dozen new German fighter planes that took control. The EEF suffered nearly fifty percent casualties until, hurt and discouraged, they were withdrawn back into their Egyptian defensive line. Ultimately London would decide that having twice snatched defeat from the jaws of victory, General Murray would have to go and soon. He would be brought home, given medals and a promotion, and spend the rest of the war in charge of a training depot.

The conflicts within the ranks of the British command staff in Cairo became even more acute during this spring of setback and confusion. Nowhere was this division sharper than between the senior planners on Murray's staff and Clayton's Eastern Mediterranean Special Intelligence Bureau (EMSIB) officers in the Savoy. This schism could easily be called a conflict between supporters of Aaron Aaronsohn's plan to seize Palestine and those who clung to the Arab Revolt. Welding the many Arab tribes into a serious asset was considered a more cost-effective use of limited resources to maximum effect. In that spring of 1917, the Arab Revolt advocates used the example of T.E. Lawrence as proof they were right.

T.E. Lawrence, Cairo Barracks (1917)

The transformation of Thomas Edward Lawrence from a talented but little-regarded writer of articles for Arab Bureau publications to a charismatic folk hero caused many of the Zionist sympathizers to deride him. Both Walter Gribbon and the controversial ornithologist and desert spy Richard Meinertzhagen dismissed him after the war as an "imposter" and "fraud." That view glosses over the facts that during his 1916–1917 sojourns among the desert Arabs, Lawrence was brave, daring, and skilled at the problematic task of welding the rivalry-ridden Arab leadership into a credible fighting force.

Once Lawrence received his honors degree in history in 1910, Hogarth took his career in hand and landed him a summer job at an archaeological exploration sponsored by the British Museum. This was followed from 1911 through 1913 on a project sponsored by the museum digging for antiquities and mapping parts of the mammoth abandoned Hittite city of Carchemish. It was there that he became friends with Stewart Newcombe and Leonard Woolley and brushed up against Gertrude Bell who had staked her own claim nearby.

Once again, Lawrence shifted his focus and identity. During the seasons at Carchemish, he abandoned his interest in the crusading knights and became entranced with the more romantic image of the desert Arab tribes and their fierce codes of honor and survival in that harsh land. He would have happily spent his life studying them and their customs. But the impending outbreak of war in the summer of 1914 put an end to that dream and to the Carchemish project.

He was turned down for military service because of his size, but Hogarth rescued him to be part of an intelligence team for the British High Command in Cairo along with Newcombe and Woolley. While he was not pleased to be regarded as a junior staffer when the group was assembled as the Arab Bureau, Lawrence had the opportunity to shift his identity again as a spy, and starting in the autumn of 1916, as a leader of an Arab guerrilla force.

During the last months of 1916 and the first months of 1917, Lawrence gained influence with Sharif Hussein and convinced him to halt efforts at capturing the holy city of Medina, but rather to merely lay siege to it and thus tie up a large Turkish force that could be used at Gaza. Then he gained kudos and later a boost to his legend by directing the band led by Prince Faisal to repeatedly attack the vital railroad tracks across the Hejaz desert, which the Turks needed to supply their garrison at Medina. Those raids took even more Turkish manpower to repair and protect.

By late in the spring of 1917, Lawrence was no longer a mere staff clerk but a major addition to the British staff clique who believed that the Arabs should be given postwar control (under British–French supervision) over Syria–Palestine, with no important role planned for its Jewish people.

For Ormsby-Gore, Deedes, and Gribbon (who was now in Egypt), it was necessary for the pro-Zionists on the staff to counter the recent apparent triumphs Lawrence was reporting back from the desert. They needed to come up with a hero figure of their own. While Aaron was certainly an authoritative personality, there was growing gossip and curiosity about his sister, who was directing the "A Organization's" activities inside Palestine.

Aaron was agreeable. For weeks, he had been urging Sarah to come to Cairo and safety, and leave the running of NILI to Josef Lishansky. But in the aftermath of Murray's failure at the first attack on Gaza, Djamal Pasha in a fit of rage blamed Jewish saboteurs and spies for the fact that the British had almost succeeded. His order to expel all the Jews of Jaffa and Tel Aviv sent shockwaves through Syria–Palestine.

With studied cruelty, he further forbade those to be expelled from seeking shelter in either Jerusalem or Haifa. The wealthy, he stated, could join their families elsewhere, the poor would be provided for (he promised) in desert camps in northern Syria. It was clear this was the beginning of a pogrom whose scope and savagery would know no limits.

He gloated in Turkish newspapers, "I know the Jewish community in Palestine is waiting for the English like a bride is waiting for a bridegroom, but as the bridegroom comes closer, we will move the bride farther away."

More than a thousand refugees flooded into Zichron Ya'akov alone. Those who had relatives were taken in, but the rest were herded into the communal barns and warehouses. Food was already scarce but now the threat of starvation and disease was compounded by the real fear that Djamal's wrath would fall on them all.

From the south, Naaman Belkind sent reports combined with Sarah's that were the first break through the total news blackout Turkish censorship had imposed after the two battles for Gaza. Aaron took the information and used it to produce a report, which was sent to the Eastern Mediterranean Special Intelligence Bureau, then up the command chain to political officials like Mark Sykes and on to the Foreign Office and Lloyd George in London. It detailed how the Jewish residents of Jaffa and Tel Aviv had been driven from their homes with no notice, and were forced to flee after being robbed of the few possessions they had been able to take with them. Those who had relatives in other villages had to make their way on foot; others were herded into makeshift concentration camps in the desert wasteland and left to perish. Those who had tried to resist were hanged from lampposts to hasten the rest.

Aaron also passed the report to a Reuters news service reporter who made worldwide headlines with it. Before the Turks could produce their own version of the events, the NILI version had an immediate impact in those tense days just before President Wilson decided to take America into the war. Spurred by the outcry from influential Jewish allies of the president, the State Department filed angry protests to both the German and Turkish embassies. Berlin quickly advised the two Pashas in Constantinople to rein in their colleague from further attacks on the Jews in Palestine, at least for the time being.

Back in Zichron Ya'akov, Sarah could know none of this and the cloud of fear continued to hang over them all. If she came to Cairo she could bear dramatic personal witness to the horrors and help arouse the British command to hasten its liberating invasion. Arrangements were made for her to come on the next visit of the *Managem*, but Aaron gave strict orders that both Josef Lishansky and Liova Schneersohn were to remain behind to keep the NILI network providing the increasing flow of intelligence being ordered by EMSIB.

But Lishansky would not hear of staying behind. For all of his energy, intellect, and bravery, he was turning out to be an increasing security danger. The twenty-seven-year-old Lishansky had a long history of courting controversy, for one so young.

He had been an early member of the *Ha-Shomer* force that rivaled the Gideonites, but he had been expelled when he killed an Arab in a brawl and had to escape to the south. *Ha-Shomer* had once been just the farm protectors organized by the *Second Aliyah* hardliners. Since then it had transformed into a clandestine paramilitary wing of an alliance between the young militant Zionists and the establishment old Yishuv communities. In their eyes, Lishansky was a dangerous traitor and his identification with NILI and the Aaronsohns made them all potential targets of reprisal and denunciation. They also resented his now distributing some of the aid relief funds that Aaron was able to send from abroad. A showdown between the two forces loomed during this time of crisis and fear.

Worse, Lishansky bruised the feelings of some of the early Gideonite-NILI operatives, who were putting themselves in peril to get the raw data and hand it over to him with little thanks. When he had first returned from Cairo, Sarah had sent him north to try to recruit new spies—as well as new contacts—from previous friends within *Ha-Shomer*. But he had taken some of the gold meant for relief work and outfitted himself in new suits, and his bragging manner had offended most of the contacts he approached. In Zichron Ya'akov itself he had become a figure of gossip and suspicion. What was he up to with Sarah, traveling so much, doing who-knew-what? Sarah's own brother Zvi was increasingly and vocally resentful that Lishansky, and not he, was second in command of NILI. He also was offended at Lishansky's open attempts to flirt with his sister. When Naaman Belkind came north to press for more information about the fate of Absalom, Zvi horrified the impressionable youth by telling him he suspected Lishansky of betraying, perhaps even murdering, his beloved cousin in order to replace him.

Despite Aaron's adamant orders, and against Sarah's wishes, when the date for her departure drew near, Josef insisted on going with her to Cairo. He would not take no for an answer. The conflict grew even worse when Liova announced that if Josef went, he would go as well. Zvi could take charge at Athlit. For most of this time Liova's love for Sarah had confined itself to writing sentimental poems to her and following her around like a pet, but he was not about to let her go off alone with the man he considered his rival. It was a catastrophe in the making, and Sarah was powerless to prevent it.

Sarah's rationale was that she would stay in Cairo only a few days, meet with Aaron, and settle some problems of how to respond to demands from Yishuv officials for control of the increasing flow of American and British gold that was coming to her. Then she would return while the moon was still in its dark phase. Zvi surely could handle whatever came up during that time. Without saying, she also wanted to get the real story from Aaron about what had happened to Absalom. Josef clearly was grieving but there were parts of his tale that troubled her. Had he really stayed with the dying Absalom while being pursued by the Bedouin, or had he abandoned him? And how much longer could she be expected to keep Absalom's death a secret from his family and his NILI comrades?

On the night of April 16, 1917, even as the second attack on Gaza was underway, the *Managem* anchored off Athlit, and Sarah, Josef, and Liova boarded with their leather bags of intelligence. A day later, they docked at Port Said and Aaron was on the port boat that came out to meet them. There was joy at being reunited with his beloved sister, but it quickly turned to towering rage when Aaron saw Josef as well as Liova. They argued that since the trip was just for three days or so, no harm could come to NILI. But Aaron had a longer stay in mind and, once ashore, turned on Josef in violent anger at this disruption in his plans.

By this time Aaron finally was getting recognition by General Murray's personal staff, and the commander himself, for having uniquely valuable expertise and strategic insight about Palestine. Until spurred by London to shift emphasis from relying on Arab allies to drive the Turks from the eastern desert regions of the Ottoman territory, the level of ignorance about Palestine at headquarters was astonishing. While there were knowledgeable Zionists like Sykes, Gribbon, and Ormsby-Gore, many of Murray's advisers were surprised to learn of the size and spread of Jewish settlements in what was assumed to be an Arab land.

While the commanding general increasingly invited Aaron to give personal briefings, he was still not quite ready to change his strategy in the Gaza campaigns, which seemed so close to victory only to fall short with heavy losses. Murray listened to, but rejected, two detailed plans that Aaron proposed as alternatives to repeated frontal assaults on Gaza's city fortifications. One was to launch an amphibious assault on the Palestine coast just south of Haifa. With the Gallipoli disaster still bitter in British memories, that was rejected out of hand. The second, a flank attack on Beersheba to capture its vast wells and then use portable drills and pumps to water the troops and animals in the march through the desert, was dismissed as too complicated. Murray, a sensitive soul, tried to placate Aaron by promising to make him minister of agricultural affairs for all of Syria–Palestine and Mesopotamia if and when the British drove the Turks away.

Despite this disappointment, Aaron was greatly encouraged by what he saw as increased influence, and began putting in ten-hour days at the Savoy Hotel staff offices and then working into the early morning hours. He completely rewrote the army's official, and highly secret, briefing book for line officers on Palestine. Many of the maps and descriptions of places had not been updated since the first British surveys of thirty years before, and some data were glaringly wrong. He began to get grudging praise from officers who until recently had sneered at this presumptuous Jewish spy.

Because of his increased workload and sense of urgency, he was annoyed when Sarah pressed him about Absalom's fate. He abruptly told her he accepted Josef's story. Moreover, an Australian cavalry patrol had questioned Bedouin spotted near the site of the gunfight, and was convinced that Absalom had not been abandoned and captured. It was still troubling that the shallow grave the tribesmen said they dug for his body could not be found. They would just have to accept that their beloved comrade was dead and struggle on.

While Aaron was glad enough to have Sarah safely in Cairo, he also became annoyed at all the attention she received from British officers who came to the Savoy headquarters and to the Continental's lobby for a look at this rumored Jewish spy heroine who was becoming something of a mythic figure at headquarters. And Aaron was even more annoyed at how Josef and Liova dogged her footsteps everywhere she went, neither letting the other be alone with her.

Sarah herself was very unhappy in Cairo. She was ill from recurring bouts of malarial fever and weak from malnourishment and stress, and she had shocked Aaron with how much weight she'd lost and how pale her normally healthy complexion had become. Nor was Cairo any more attractive to her than Constantinople had been even though they all dined out, attended the theater, and were feted by the wealthier Jewish émigrés there. While she tolerated the rivalry between her two would-be lovers, she found the attention of the British officers embarrassing since she spoke no English.

When no less a skeptic than Captain Edmonds visited them at the Continental Hotel to express the high regard the command had for her work, she replied in icy French that if he was truly grateful he could arrange an instant boat trip back to Athlit. She did not, as some have written, meet Lawrence as he was deep in the desert planning the daring raid on the strategic Red Sea port of Aqaba that would burnish his myth.

Finally in mid-May, Aaron agreed to arrange a trip home for the trio on the *Managem*. He had become worried at the state of NILI operations and ordered to dramatically increase the flow of information from the group, now that the Gaza offensive had failed. Even more important, his work spreading international alarm over the travails of the Jews of Jaffa had sparked a flood of aid money from America and Britain, and those funds were desperately needed back in Palestine. He also recognized that the rivalry between Josef and Liova was turning into dangerous enmity that could cause real trouble when they had to work together at Athlit.

Indeed, just as the three were to board the ship at Port Said, Lishansky went into a temper tantrum and threatened not to go back. It took three days of cajoling until finally, on May 17, the *Managem* sailed within sight of the Athlit station but could not land Sarah and the others because of a sudden storm. They returned and languished in Port Said for another two weeks. During that time Josef was occupied with a British training course on explosives. The British wanted NILI to destroy a vital railroad bridge that crossed the Jordan River and brought essential supplies to the Turkish front near Beersheba. When his instructor offered Josef a £100 bonus for undertaking the mission, he threw another temper tantrum.

Finally the three set sail and, again, were prevented by weather from getting ashore. This time the resentful captain insisted that the ship complete its other assigned patrol and then return, not to Egypt but to the big Royal Navy base at Famagusta, Cyprus.

Two more sweltering weeks were wasted at anchor in Famagusta, where the trio was forbidden to go ashore. Two months after they had set out for Cairo, the *Managem* anchored off Athlit on June 15, and sent Sarah and the others ashore with a sizable store of provisions that included large sacks containing fifty thousand gold French franc coins that, along with British gold sovereigns, were the only acceptable hard currency in that desperate region. It was a literal lifesaver for the starving Jewish communities now choked with refugees from Jaffa and other cities where Turkish oppression had become insupportable.

The gold turned out to be more than a lifesaver for the communities; it arrived just in time to prevent a complete collapse of the NILI organization. During Sarah's two-month absence, her brother Zvi had been unable to effectively command the widespread network and keep it working. Worse, her disappearance caused gossip to circulate that she had run off with Lishansky, and joined her other siblings in a life of luxury with the British.

Zvi, despite his jealousy of Lishansky's senior role, lacked both his energy and willingness to take risks. He panicked when he and Ephraim were visited by a delegation from the security committee of the Yishuv organization. These elders pointedly accused the Aaronsohns of putting all the Jews in Palestine at risk of extermination with their dangerous spying. Colonel Aziz Bek had shifted his counterespionage efforts from quashing Arab subversion to a full-time probe of the Jewish population, and he was known to be making pointed inquiries of a possible spy ring somewhere south of Haifa.

When the elders threatened to denounce the Athlit station to Colonel Bek, Zvi panicked and despite Ephraim's advice, promised to urge Sarah to dismantle NILI as soon as she returned. The wave of fear throughout the Yishuv also had its effect on NILI operatives everywhere. To add to his miseries, Naaman Belkind had become increasingly unwilling to accept the fantasy about Absalom being in England. Lishansky's disappearance merely fed Belkind's suspicion that he had murdered his cousin to take his place in Sarah's affections.

So despite her fatigue and alarm at how NILI had deteriorated, Sarah threw herself into trying to set things right. She made effective use of the gold and won a grudging reprieve from the Yishuv by letting them take charge of much of the money and distribute it. She also sent Josef traveling to revive the network and the flow of current intelligence.

This began NILI's most productive time. The courier ship now came on a dependable schedule, but the most current data on troop movements were entrusted to the homing pigeons that were often launched six at a time with capsules of enciphered messages in Hebrew script. Replacements were regularly brought ashore with each ship visit, and Sarah and Liova spent hours encoding and transcribing as soon as the intelligence arrived.

By this time General Murray had been recalled to Britain, loaded with promotions and medals. On June 27, his replacement, General Edmund Allenby, arrived, and one of the first people he asked to see was Aaron Aaronsohn.

Allenby was the very idea of a fighting general, to Prime Minister Lloyd George. A veteran cavalry officer, Allenby had risen in notoriety and criticism at Western Front battles at Ypres and the Somme. His strategy was always to counterattack whenever the Germans launched an offensive. His casualty lists were horrendous and his troops called him "Bloody Bull" for erupting into a towering rage at any miscarriage of his orders. But his soldiers fought for him because he paid special attention to their support and care whenever they were not on the attack.

Before he sailed for Cairo he had been given Aaron's original report plus the more recent memos that Clayton's aides had drafted. In the first week of July, Lawrence and a band of Howeitat captured Aqaba and added to the rekindling of optimism in Cairo. So which strategy would this new commander choose? Faced with the Arab–Zionist division of opinion within his command, Allenby broke the impasse by choosing both strategies. The Arab uprising would be used to distract the Turks at Gaza, while the real attack would begin where Aaron had advised, against Beersheba on the eastern flank. As a condition to taking the command, he had won grudging assent from London for a fresh supply of troops and heavy weapons that would be siphoned away from France.

Allenby had promised Lloyd George to meet his demand to capture Jerusalem by Christmas, and he did not intend to fail.

CHAPTER TEN

The Net Closes

•••••••••••••••••••••

July–December 1917

Lawrence in a posed costume, ca. 1919

Lawrence and Gertrude Bell, Cairo, 1917

The net began to close on Sarah and NILI, even as General Allenby moved his headquarters in Cairo closer to the front in early August. The new commander firmly believed in personally overseeing the build-up for the all-out attack on Gaza based on Aaron's strategy. The whole region from Cairo to Beirut was in ferment in the late summer of 1917. The commanders of the opposing armies were braced for what would be the final struggle. In the Jewish settlements of Palestine there was the heightened despair that even if they survived the carnage of the impending battle, the threat of starvation could destroy them just the same.

More than anyone else, Sarah was operating at stress levels that could not be sustained for long. Bouts of malarial fever and malnutrition had sapped her strength. The workload was crushing. She now had two dozen full-time agents and a network of roughly twice that number of auxiliaries—sources of occasional but often vitally important intelligence. Spread from Damascus to Jerusalem, most of the full-time agents were former Gideonites and personal loyalists. The others often held positions of trust—and thus of equal danger—as civilian workers for the Turkish government or armed forces: clerks, telephone operators, physicians. These required a steady infusion of money to compensate for the risks they took. While the NILI needed no bribes, they had expenses, too.

The simple logistics of getting intelligence from its source—a code clerk at Turkish headquarters in Damascus—back to Athlit, and from there to Cairo, was an increasing nightmare for Sarah and Josef Lishansky. Travel by railroad was expensive and the roads were in an advancing stage of decay because of the Turks' movement of heavy artillery back and forth, and their neglect of any maintenance.

Most worrying was the increase in Turkish patrols, and reports Sarah received that there had been inquiries by the authorities suspicious of a spy ring operating among the Jews. NILI had other problems. While both the British and French operated independent spy operations throughout Syria–Palestine, these were uncoordinated and only occasionally fruitful. Yet they left footprints that aroused suspicions of the Turks. Only NILI was still completely undetected—but not for much longer.

Sarah reported to Aaron, "We are under increasing surveil-lance. Patrols stop travelers everywhere and more often now bribes do not work and there are more arrests. But we continue."

Djamal Pasha's chief of counterintelligence, Colonel Aziz Bek, had become so alarmed at the specter of a Jewish spy plot that could turn into their version of the Arab Revolt, that he moved the headquarters of his counterintelligence corps from Damascus to Jerusalem that summer. He had evidence that the army's band of coast watchers were worse than useless drunkards who rarely patrolled, despite frequent reports of strange ships at anchor offshore in the dark of night.

He had a personal motive as well as his official duty: He despised Djamal Pasha for his ineptitude and greed, and also for his dissolute taste for Jewish women. He had received reports that Djamal had even propositioned a woman named Sarah Aar-onsohn when she stayed at the Fast Hotel in Jerusalem earlier that summer. He had known both Aaron and Sarah when they visited Djamal and attended social gatherings in Damascus ear-lier in the war. He resented their influence with his commander. Since Aaron was reported to have vanished, he made a note to investigate the sister further.

Meanwhile the pressure on Sarah and NILI to deliver an increasing flow of real-time intelligence grew exponentially, as General Allenby and his new cadre of commanders pushed to complete plans and position their troops for the final assault on Gaza and the vital coast road running northward. The schedule was to attack early in September. The plan was based on one Aaron had been arguing for since his arrival in Cairo in 1916. The capture of Beersheba with its vast underground reservoirs on the far eastern flank of the Turkish positions was to be followed by a quick capture of successive villages, where in Biblical times there had been ample subsurface wells that the engineers could drill and pump back into existence.

Water was every bit as vital to the British offensive as firepower. Most of the troops of the Australian and New Zealand forces that were to attack the eastern flank were mounted, and virtually all of the artillery and support vehicles were horse-drawn. While the ANZAC troopers were jokingly said to exist on their beer rations, the animals could not. Aaron spent much of July on scouting missions with ANZAC engineers spotting where the likely wells and springs could be found, while Allenby rushed into constructing a water filtration plant capable of purifying six hundred thousand gallons of water a day and a pipeline to carry water from the Nile all the way to the forward British lines. Once the force pushed ahead on the attack, it would be up to Aaron's wells to carry them across the desert so they could flank the Turkish positions at Gaza. Aaron also advised bringing sufficient pipes to bring fresh water to Jerusalem whose supplies had been ruined by Turkish mismanagement.

To the horror of the Arab Bureau staff and Arabists at headquarters, Aaron also was advising Allenby and his political strategists about how the Jews of Palestine could be an important part of the British administration of the region after the Turks were forced out. Since the Arabists (with explicit permission of the Lloyd George government) had promised both Sharif Hussein of Mecca (and it was hoped, Medina) and Ibn Saud, chief of the Wahhabi Arabs of Riyadh, that each would be the sovereign over all of Syria–Palestine, the idea of sharing any of the region with the Jews was unthinkable.

"Aaronsohn is running HQ these days," complained an irritated Captain Edmonds in a letter to a friend. Lawrence was more than irritated when he arrived in Cairo in August flush with his success at Aqaba. Newly promoted to captain, Lawrence was affronted to learn there was now a new plan for the administration of Palestine that rivaled his own. Aaron recorded their first of many confrontations in his diary on August 12.

> *I had a chat with Captain Lawrence this morning. Our interview was devoid of amenity. He has been too successful at an early age—and is infatuated with himself. He gave me a lesson on our colonies—the mentality of the people—the feelings (sentiment) of the Arabs, etc., etc. As I was listening to him I could almost imagine that I was attending a conference by a scientific anti-Semitic Prussian speaking English. I am afraid the German spirit has taken deeper root in the minds of pastors and archaeologists.*
>
> *One would gather from the above interview that nothing can be done in Judea and Samaria where Faisal will never gain access. There might be something to do in Galilea. But Lawrence will conduct his investigation by his own methods in order to learn of the mentality of the Jews in Galilean colonies. If they are in favor of the Arabs they will be spared, otherwise they will have their throats cut. He is still at the age where people do not doubt themselves—happy young man! He is plainly hostile to us. He must be of missionary breed.*

While Aaron was well aware that Sarah and NILI were in increasing danger, he was so preoccupied with expanding his influence with Allenby and the ascendant Zionists on the staff, that all he did in those final weeks of summer was urge Sarah to board the *Managem* as soon as possible and come to Cairo. That she could not and would not do. It would be a betrayal of the other NILI agents and put her remaining family members in peril, not to mention threaten Zichron Ya'akov as well.

All the while Sarah was handling an ever-increasing demand by the British for more detailed and more current intelligence on where the Turkish and German troops were being moved, and the location of new fortifications. NILI produced a huge volume of vital data in response, astonishing given the logistical obstacles in their path.

On several occasions their reports of new construction for trench lines and artillery emplacements allowed British bombers to destroy the projects. Before long, Sarah's operatives had provided Allenby with what is known as an order of battle—a list of every German and Turkish unit, the number of effective troops in each unit, the amount and kinds of weapons, and numbers and types of artillery, as well as the names of the regimental commanders and their exact positions and what their orders were. No general ever went on the attack with a better grasp of his enemy and his strength.

Even in her time of triumph Sarah's life began to unravel. She was continually vexed by Josef Lishansky's growing instability. She suspected he was pilfering sums of the aid money he was supposed to be distributing to communities in dire need of support, and spending it on showy new suits and neckties. He was already an anathema to his former *Ha-Shomer* compatriots, although she firmly believed him innocent of accusations that he had murdered an Arab. The result was that Josef could no longer risk traveling about the region gathering intelligence from the operatives in the field. He was effectively confined to Zichron Ya'akov and, finally, his presence there began to cause problems.

To her alarm, her brother Zvi believed the *Ha-Shomer*

charges and, worse, believed Josef had murdered Absalom as well. Zvi had a longstanding complaint: Aaron, Absalom, and Alexander had implemented the NILI ring without consulting him. And he was infuriated that Sarah had not turned to him to be second in command of NILI, even though he had been only a part-time operative from the start. He put them all in danger by passing on his suspicions to the childlike Naaman Belkind, who was deeply devoted to his cousin Absalom and increasingly suspicious at his disappearance.

Naaman had produced a great deal of good intelligence from his southern vantage point at Rishon-le-Zion. But he treated the task as a game and took reckless risks. He used the village's wine supplies to curry favor with German and even Turkish officers, and made deliveries as far as the headquarters at Beersheba where he openly asked suspicious questions. For the moment, the officers treated him as a naïve and sometimes annoying clown—but one still welcome for the wine he freely dispensed.

Zvi finally became convinced that NILI under Sarah and Josef endangered the family as well as the community. While Ephraim had known about what his children were doing, Zvi convinced him that the risks were now too great. In August, as their fears grew, a Zichron village council sent some elders to them, and later demanded to see Sarah.

When Sarah met with the elders, they informed her that her conduct with the married Lishansky was scandalous in itself. They also were convinced that she and Lishansky engaged in dangerous spying for the British and put the whole community, indeed all of the Jewish settlements, in extreme peril. Had she not seen with her own eyes what the Turks did to the Armenians? Did she not see her home village jammed with refugees from Djamal Pasha's expulsion of Jews from Jaffa and Tel Aviv? Did she really believe these British were going to liberate Palestine from the Turks—and even if it were true, at what cost?

Believing that Allenby's attack was days away, Sarah stalled for time. Without admitting anything, she agreed that she and Josef would stop staying in the house on Founders Street and stay out at Athlit. Moreover, she vaguely promised to begin scaling back some of her activities. She needed time, she said, for were they not aware that she had been distributing a great deal of needed relief money, much of it going into their own hands? Grumbling, the elders went away but not before ominously warning her that if she did not stop spying, they might denounce her to the Turks. As it turned out, the threat was more than ominous.

Then, toward the end of August, a series of actions by the British began to fatally undermine the safety of Sarah and the entire NILI network. There is a suspicion among some early historians of the Aaronsohn saga that some of those mistakes were intentionally undertaken by Aaron's enemies among the Arabists at the Savoy headquarters. A more charitable, but just as unprovable, interpretation is that the British were so preoccupied with the run-up to the Third Battle of Gaza that they got careless. The consequences were fatal nonetheless.

First, there was a security failure regarding the gold sovereign coins delivered by the *Managem* in heavy leather sacks. Sarah had long ago handed over the forty thousand French francs to the central council of the Yishuv and its *Ha-Shomer* force for distribution to the starving Jewish villages that needed to buy food and pay bribes to their increasingly rapacious Arab neighbors. The British gold to support NILI operations amounted to a few hundred pounds a month—paltry when compared to the hundreds of thousands of pounds Lawrence and others were paying to Hussein and Saud—but it was vital. For one thing, it kept the elders of Zichron Ya'akov from taking any action that would disrupt flow of aid to them.

The British and French had maintained a tight blockade of the Syria–Palestine coast since early 1915, therefore basic security protocol demanded that no gold given to Sarah should show mint marks later than 1914. But Colonel Bek's operatives began picking up sovereign coins minted in 1916, and that could only mean that the enemy was operating a more formidable spy operation in his territory than had been suspected.

Then there were the pigeons. For Sarah the pigeons had been a nuisance from the start. Scarce materials had to be used to build a dovecote as specified in the army manual that came with the first shipment. Even scarcer grain had to be supplied to feed the birds, and workers had to be diverted to keep the birds clean and fed. While Allenby's army used radio telegraphs and had an extensive field telephone system connected to headquarters, the final maneuvers and scouting made increasing use of their own pigeons to connect with more distant outposts.

In those final weeks when the demand for information rose exponentially, the replacement birds provided the Athlit station were clearly not well trained. Some refused to leave the dovecote at all. Others flew a short distance and returned. Some just disappeared.

One morning in early September, the Moudir, the chief of police for Caesarea just south of Athlit, rose early and after prayers and a cup of tea he followed his custom and went into his garden in his robe to feed and admire his flock of homing pigeons. He was extremely proud of his birds but that morning he noticed a strange pigeon had landed at the coop to feed.

Curious, he picked up the bird and saw it had a small rubber capsule fixed to one leg. He removed it and prying it open, found a tightly wound ribbon of fragile paper. As he unrolled it he saw it was a series of Hebrew letters that he suspected at once of being some kind of cipher he could not translate. He sent it at once to Colonel Aziz Bek, and when his staff could not unscramble the message it was rushed by courier to Constantinople. While the message could not be deciphered there either, Bek got immediate and explicit orders—find the Jewish spy ring operating so blatantly in his jurisdiction, and do it at once.

The spymasters of the EMSIB in Cairo began to get sloppy with their own network of spies in the area. Two young Christian Palestinians were immediately rounded up after being put ashore north of Haifa. A Jesuit priest was denounced and arrested in possession of some of the later mint sovereigns. Tortured, they all quickly admitted their spying, and further confirmed that there was yet another spy ring operated by Jews farther south. Bek's focus narrowed, and he flooded the area between Haifa and Caesarea with his own agents and mounted gendarmerie who went from village to village to question terrified residents.

Sarah was soon aware of these disasters, and her letters to Aaron reflected her growing fears that the Turks were closing in on her and NILI. As a precaution, she destroyed the remaining pigeons and buried them. She also began to hide her caches of gold and documents—either by burying them near the station or in one of the caves that dotted the Carmel mountain range.

Aaron, however, was increasingly preoccupied with a problem that had vexed him from the time he left London a year before. Chaim Weizmann and the overarching World Zionist Organization had steadfastly refused to show any partiality for either the Allies or the German-led Central Powers. They were playing a longer game to secure an independent Jewish homeland in Palestine. Waiting to see who would win the terrible European conflict seemed only prudent.

Adding to the complexity of the Zionist posture was that the British and French were busy fleshing out the details of the secret Sykes–Picot pact that aimed to divide Syria-Palestine between them. Weizmann knew what Aaron did not: there was now an agreement that part of Palestine would include a protectorate for the Jews under British control. At the same time, the Turks and the Kaiser's diplomats were dangling the prospect of a semi-autonomous zone for the Jewish settlements in Palestine if the Central Powers won. The Zionist officials had to wait and see which side would prevail. The American troops had landed in France but had not yet turned the tide of battle. The Germans could still win.

The central council of the Yishuv excitedly got word to Weizmann that no less than Djamal Pasha had suddenly left his command to journey to Berlin for joint German–Turkish talks with Jewish officials in Berlin. No one could know that the talks were basically a sham to keep the WZO from suddenly bolting to the Allied side. As it turned out, the assignment of Djamal Pasha to the talks was engineered by General von Kressenstein, the Fourth Army field commander, to keep Djamal from interfering during the expected battle over Gaza.

Aaron found all this temporizing infuriating. Equally frustrating was the fact that Weizmann refused to permit Aaron to administer some of the funds being raised by Jewish donors in America and Britain for the relief of the starving villages in Palestine. After all, it was NILI that alerted the world to Djamal Pasha's expulsion of Jews from Jaffa and Tel Aviv. And Rivka, still in New York, had taken a leadership role in raising donations from wealthy American Jews—even those who were still skeptics about Zionism.

He sent a series of telegrams begging Weizmann to release funds to help with the expenses of his Cairo activities and to prompt the WZO to publicly back the Allies, but they had gone unanswered for most of the year. Until the last week of August the British had also forbidden Aaron to go to London to confront his adversary, but then just as suddenly Deedes informed him he was to board a ship for England with just twenty-four hours' notice. Again, some historians have suspected the British wanted him out of the way on the eve of the attack.

Aaron had sent ahead a lengthy letter by courier to Weizmann, setting up the confrontation. In ornately formal French, the language of scientific publications, Aaron urged him,

> The declaration of neutrality on the part of official Zionism seemed to me since the start of the war like vulgar opportunism, in other words, an attitude that is both lacking in dignity and unpolitical. There is no shadow of a doubt that from the points of feeling, conviction, and Realpolitik we need to follow the Allies, whatever the results of the struggle. . . . I wait with anxiety new decisions by you that are inspired and reflect these new conditions. I am an optimistic Jew. And I have confidence in your high intelligence and I hope that your decisions will be the best for our cause. I hope for a true confidence and collaboration between us and no further suborning of my efforts.

Anxious to resolve this frustration, Aaron rushed to sail for London. He left behind his brothers Alexander and Shmuel, who had come from America to help translate the intelligence flow in Hebrew and in code. Both men had been given instant officer commissions and uniforms, and swaggered about the hotels. The

British flattered them and made much over Alex and his experiences in the Turkish army. Aaron gave Alex firm instructions to convince Sarah to leave NILI in Lishansky's control and flee to Cairo and safety. But he did little other than send a few perfunctory messages, which she ignored.

Like everyone else in Palestine, Sarah was waiting for the imminent British attack. But the first weeks of September came and went with no sign of it. General Allenby apparently had taken one of Aaron's early briefing papers to heart. The memo warned that the period of August and September was the most dangerous season for malarial fevers. He decided to wait well into October before launching the offensive. Meanwhile he had succeeded in getting London to divert added units from France to Egypt, and used the time to strengthen his force.

Allenby might have had the luxury of waiting, but the Jews of Palestine were near the breaking point as their spirits were crushed between worsening privation and the brutality of the Turkish spy-hunters prowling around them. Longstanding resentments among the Aaronsohns' neighbors at Zichron turned into anger. How dare that family put the whole community in such peril?

Naaman Belkind's caution finally gave way. Early in September, he recklessly convinced a young Albanian officer in the Turkish army to defect. The unhappy soldier was a frequent consumer of Naaman's generous gifts of wine. Importantly, he was the secretary to a Turkish commander, and had accompanied him on an inspection tour of the new trenches being dug around Beersheba. Naaman bragged that he need not risk escaping across the desert to the British lines. He belonged to a group that had regular contact by sea and would take him to Athlit on the next boat scheduled to call. To Sarah and Josef's horror, he suddenly showed up at Athlit with the officer, who had taken four days leave from his post. Unhappily, the ship did not appear and Josef had to hide him with NILI allies in Haifa until he could be taken away.

Naaman was bitter when, instead of praise for his coup, both Sarah and Josef rebuked him sharply for his foolishness and they dismissed his renewed demands that he be allowed to go to Cairo to find Absalom. Zvi was now demanding that Sarah send Aaron his own letters accusing Josef of murdering Absalom and seducing his sister. Further poisoned by Zvi's bitterness, Naaman could no longer endure his suspicions about his cousin's fate, so he decided to try to follow him and cross the desert to Cairo and put his doubts to rest. Without telling anyone, he left Rishon-le-Zion and set out—only to be quickly arrested by the Turks and taken to the police compound at Beersheba. There, the German officers demanded that he be hanged at once. But the Turks had plans for Naaman.

An infantry colonel who had been one of Naaman's best wine customers made a big show of rescuing him from the Germans and soothing his fears. He held a lavish dinner in Naaman's honor and plied him with his own wine infused with hashish. The gullible young man, now drugged and euphoric, became expansive and boastful.

The Turkish colonel hinted that he too was fed up with military service, and understood that the British paid bounties to Turkish officers of his rank—which he would be glad to share with his friend. Naaman bragged that he knew how to get them both to Cairo: by embarking on a British vessel that called on friends of his on the coast. While he may not have named Sarah explicitly, he provided enough clues for Aziz Bek to make the connection. The Turkish warders tortured Naaman brutally to extract whatever other information they could, and then he was bundled off to the prison in Damascus to await trial and likely execution for his recklessness. Once in the Damascus main prison, worse tortures awaited him.

News of Naaman's arrest spread panic through NILI's ranks. It was time for Sarah to flee, but roadblocks and raids made it impossible for NILI to function. The Turks had begun to arrest suspects in other villages, some not even privy to NILI's existence. Zichron Ya'akov was paralyzed by an intolerable fear of extermination and it was only a matter of time before someone would break and inform on her and the band.

When the *Managem* made its next visit to Athlit on September 25, it carried a letter from Alexander urging her to leave everything in Josef's hands and come at once to Cairo. But Sarah was adamant. She would only come to Cairo for a brief stay until the British invasion was underway. And Josef must come with her. But when the ship anchored, Josef suffered a bout of malarial fever. She would not leave without him. Instead, she sent the Turkish officer and some relatives, including Shmuel's wife and child in her place. She told the courier that they were to come for them both in two days. By then she would have shut down the NILI network, gotten everyone to safety, Josef would have recovered enough from his fever to get into the rescue skiff with her, and she could leave with a clear conscience.

But the *Managem* did not return and some have wondered at the British failure. Alexander would later write in his memoir the excuse that the *Managem*'s captain had refused because there would be a full moon in a few days and it would be too bright to escape detection. It would seem a feeble excuse for the British to have risked their most valuable intelligence source. Sarah would never know.

On September 30, with the advent of the *Sukkot* observances, Sarah abandoned hope of rescue and she and Josef returned to the house on Founders Street. Josef's wife and two children had come to Zichron Ya'akov to join in the observances. But that day, while attending a neighbor's celebration of an impending marriage, she was warned that the Turks who had been harshly questioning villages all around Zichron Ya'akov were now on their way there. She moved Josef's family to a friend's home, gave him some of their meager stash of gold and told him to hide out in one of the nearby caves. If the Turkish probe came to nothing he could return and hope for a rescue. Otherwise, he was to try to escape as best he could.

Sarah then galloped on her horse to Athlit to make sure the Arab workers were sent to their home villages with orders to deny all knowledge of what NILI had been doing. She burned the few remaining documents that had not been buried and hurried home to prepare the food for her father and brother and the festival. She was startled to find no trace of either man. Alarmed, she realized the normally busy streets of the town were empty; all of the nearby houses were tightly shuttered and dark. There was nothing to do but wait.

Just at dusk came a pounding at the door and a sergeant of the gendarmerie and two soldiers seized her and pulled her into one of the larger houses at the far end of Founders Street. Most of the rooms had been turned into jammed holding cells, for the Turks had been busy all day selectively rounding up suspects from a specific list that clearly had been provided by informants. Most were NILI loyalists, a few innocent captives—like Zvi's wife and children—were meant to be hostages to lure other suspects to surrender.

As Sarah would discover, two front rooms of the house were

set aside for the actual questioning. In the first sat Hassan Bey, the Kaimakan of Haifa and the police chief. It was here that Sarah was confronted and had to witness the savage beating of Ephraim. When he was dragged away unconscious it became her turn. While it was clear that the inquisitors were mistaken on some things—such as Ephraim's leadership of NILI—she was alarmed at how much they did know. They knew specific names of NILI agents who had escaped; most of all, they demanded to know where Josef Lishansky was hiding and when the next British boat was due to arrive.

Instead of meekly denying all knowledge, Sarah taunted them. She alone was responsible for the spying and she would live to see them all destroyed for their brutal tyranny and for the genocide of the Armenians and persecution of the Jews. Frustrated by her stubbornness, the two officials adjourned to the hotel for refreshments and had her pulled into the second room to confront the official torturer Osman Bey, one of the most feared Turks in Syria–Palestine.

The Ottomans had long perfected the techniques and use of torture as a means of extracting information and punishment. Their methods were a delicate dance of cruel brutality that inflicted maximum pain while prolonging life. Bouts of torture were alternated with periods of isolation and uncertainty to break the suspect's will. When it came to torturing women, however, the Turks had a cultural quirk that amounted to ambivalence. While it was common at the time for a Turkish man to beat his wife and other women in his household, it was considered unmanly to harm other women. The two officials did not particularly care to witness what was going to happen to Sarah, just as long as she talked.

Osman Bey, however, had no such scruples. He took pride in

the ingenuity of his craft. He tied her to a chair, as he had done with Ephraim, and beat the soles of her feet until they bled and then tore the back of her blouse to expose her back and lashed her there. He asked no questions; it was just a taste of what would come if she did not begin to talk. Then she was locked into a room where her sister-in-law, her young niece and nephew, and several other women and children were confined.

Later in the evening Sarah was dragged to the front room where Zvi's wife also was being held. To add to the unreality of the scene, all of the children were allowed by the Turks to roam freely through the house and most were oblivious to the peril they were in. Sarah immediately shouted at the officials that her sister-in-law was totally innocent of any treason and should be freed. Thinking this was a sign of her weakening, they released the woman and her children. When Sarah made it clear she would not talk further, they sent her back to Osman Bey.

But all that night and for the next three days and nights she had to withstand alternating bouts of pain and respites of fear and uncertainty. When she was not actually suffering excruciating pain herself, she had to listen to the shrieks of other prisoners from the torture room. A British intelligence report on her fate hinted strongly that she was sexually molested, even raped, by Osman Bey. That atrocity aside, Osman Bey certainly ran through his repertoire of cruelty. The beatings continued until she fainted. Single hairs were pulled from her scalp and her fingers were crushed by pliers. Near the end he boiled eggs in a spirit lamp and fixed them to scald her armpits, breasts, and, finally, into her vagina.

While this horror was going on, Hassan Bey took his search for Josef to another level. He called the Zichron Ya'akov council to the village synagogue. First, he announced a reward of fifty pounds in gold for anyone who would reveal Josef's hiding place. Then, with his second breath, he told the elders that if they did not assist him in tracking down Josef he would subject them to the same fate as the Jews of Jaffa. He would raze Zichron Ya'akov to the ground and drive them all into the desert. To their everlasting shame, the council agreed and began a search for Josef that drove him from his cave in flight to he knew not where.

Finally, on October 5, Sarah's oppressors gave up. She had not only endured everything they could subject her to, she had rebuked them with threats of her own. She is quoted as shouting at the Kaimakan and the others, "Your end is nigh, you will fall into the pit I have dug for you. You are murderers, blood-thirsty wild animals. I, a weak woman, decided to defend my people lest you do to us what you did to the Armenians. I have hated you, heroes of the *falaka* (the thin cane) and the baksheesh. . . . Osman, you hangman, what a hero you are, beating up women."

Colonel Bek's patience was exhausted as well. He ordered that Sarah be taken to Damascus, where the means of extracting information were more refined and effective. She was suddenly dragged from her isolation and put in handcuffs. Again, the complicated Turkish mores about women came into play. Sarah asked with dignity if she could be allowed to go home and change her clothing and wash her wounds before setting out. The Kaimakan was in the process of releasing many of the hostages who were no longer of use to him and perhaps he was preoccupied so he gave permission. In the process, Sarah was able to whisper to the young son of one of the hostages to come to the rear of the Aaronsohn house and search for a note she hoped to leave there and to guard it. Then he was to take it to a relative who was not a NILI, and to whom she had given some of the gold.

Then, chained between two soldiers with an armed guard

around her, Sarah walked upright and proud the length of the street to her home. From their houses her former friends and neighbors came to stare at her, and four women chased after the procession shouting abuse at her in a frenzy of suppressed fear and rage. She stared at them coldly and said nothing.

Once inside her home the macabre scene continued. She announced firmly that she intended to wash herself and change her dress in the bathroom with the door locked. After checking that she could not escape via the high window, the guards stepped out of her way. Once inside, she turned on the water tap fully, snatched up a fragment of paper and wrote a brief note that she folded up and tossed out the window.

Astonishingly, the note began with detailed orders to her relatives to pay some outstanding bills and a final wage to the Arab workers. She then reported that she had overheard her interrogators let slip the names of three informants who had betrayed her and NILI. Then she made her final plea:

> *Our situation is very bad, mine most of all because the whole blame falls on me. I was beaten murderously, and they have bound me with ropes. Do remember to describe all our suffering to those who shall come after we have passed away. I do not believe we shall survive after having been betrayed, and the whole truth about us probably exposed. The news of victory must eventually come, and as you will be seeing my brothers, tell them about our martyrdom and let them know that Sarah has asked that each drop of her blood be avenged measure for measure, vengeance upon our Jews and especially upon the rulers under whom we live that no mercy be shown, just as they have shown no mercy to us. . . .*

When the guards nervously began to call her to hurry, Sarah opened one of the bathroom cabinets and took out a small caliber pistol that Aaron had given her. She put it in her mouth and pulled the trigger. Tragically, the bullet missed her brain and instead went through her mouth and shattered her spine. When the soldiers broke open the door they rushed to call Dr. Yaffe. He later recorded in his diary, "I took some instruments and rode to the scene. I found Sarah lying unconscious on the floor of the bathroom. Next to her was a small revolver. Her pulse was faint. Blood was coming out of her mouth. I gave her a caffeine injection and her consciousness returned. She recognized me and pleaded, 'For heaven's sake, put an end to my life. I beg you, kill me . . . I can't suffer any longer. . . .'"

Yaffe rightly feared that if he did assist Sarah in dying, he himself would be executed. But putting aside his feud with Aaron, he administered morphine to ease her agony and injections of stimulants to keep her conscious. He even rebuked the Turkish military doctor who the police had insisted examine her, and extracted a promise—sincere or not—that if Sarah stabilized she would not be tortured further.

For the next three days and nights, Sarah drifted in and out of awareness. A number of women relatives and neighbors overcame their fear and kept a constant vigil at her bedside. They cooled her fever with damp cloths and called for Dr. Yaffe to return whenever her agony became unendurable. During her lucid moments she pleaded with them to make sure Ephraim and Zvi were spared further torture by the police.

At seven o'clock on the morning of October 9, a Tuesday, Sarah woke for the last time and lucidly said good-bye to the friends around her and made one last plea for them to care for her father. Then, Yaffe later wrote, "At eight-thirty she gave up her soul without revealing a thing to the Turks."

The stark reality of Sarah's end brought all of Zichron Ya'akov to its senses. The entire town followed her body wrapped in cloth to the cemetery. There, to everyone's discomfiture, the gravesite next to her mother had not been dug. It took two hours to prepare, during which the townspeople stood silently, contemplating what they had done. As the first shovels of dirt were dropped into the grave, the first rain of the autumn season began to fall.

A darkness would hang over Zichron Ya'akov for some time to come. News of the Turkish threats spread quickly, and a manhunt for Josef Lishansky began in earnest. Members of the *Ha-Shomer* joined in the pursuit. Early in his flight, Josef had been found and taken prisoner by some of his old comrades, who finally decided to let him go. On the run, out of money, he traveled by night on foot, begging handouts and a brief shelter from terrified friends. He finally made his way south to Jaffa, where in a desperate attempt to cross over to the British via the desert, he was caught trying to steal a camel.

A final irony is that during those dark weeks, Josef became something of a celebrity for the Turks. He was held for ten days in Jerusalem but not subjected to any torture. Finally, in a heavily guarded sealed railroad car he made the four-day journey to Damascus, where a crowd of Turkish officials jammed the station for a sight of this daring young man.

Once he arrived at the special jail for political prisoners, he found Naaman Belkind and a dozen NILI members. Again, Josef was not mistreated, certainly not tortured as savagely as Naaman had been. He was taken to interview Djamal Pasha, who was curious to see the fugitive.

On October 30, 1917, the Third Battle of Gaza had begun with a sweeping assault on Beersheba that sent the Turks into retreat. On the night of the thirty-first, before the Turks could maneuver eastward, a massive bombardment of Gaza began by a combined force of British and French warships anchored off-shore and a concentration of artillery. The next morning, the infantry assault on the city began.

Six days later the city was in the complete control of the British. Then followed two months of fierce fighting up the coast road as the Turks managed a doggedly skillful retreat that gave ground grudgingly. But as pledged, it was on Christmas Day, 1917, that General Allenby won a welcome from the people by entering the main gate of Jerusalem on foot as a liberator, and not on the horseback of a conqueror.

In early December there was a trial for Josef Lishansky and Naaman Belkind, but no sentence was announced. And there were rumors throughout the prison that German diplomats had urged the Three Pashas not to repeat the scandal of the Jaffa expulsions, but to treat the NILI affair as a minor matter involving a few harmless fools. They began to hope that they all might be pardoned or, at worst, draw short prison terms. After all, General Allenby had finally launched his attack.

A week, later however, Josef Lishansky and Naaman Belkind were awakened, forced into penitents' white robes, and hanged in the public square of Damascus. The crude signs hanging from their necks proclaimed them to be vile traitors. In the weeks that followed, as the Turkish troops retreated their way north in retreat, they vandalized the agriculture station at Athlit. The rooms were pillaged, the farm implements that were not stolen were wrecked, and the horses and camels of the troops were set to graze and destroy the carefully tended beds of plants.

For the time being, the flame that was Sarah Aaronsohn and NILI seemed to be extinguished. But it would not be so for long, and that flame shines as brightly today in the *Eretz Israel* that she helped bring into being thirty years later.

EPILOGUE

Myth versus History

Israeli postage stamp honoring Sarah Aaronsohn, 1991

Victors may get to write the history after great events, but it is merely a rough draft. Sarah Aaronsohn was scarcely in her grave before conflicting myths began to form, and they continue to this day. Happily, a succession of historians have begun to chip away to reveal the truth beneath the surface.

The Germans and Turks got a head start with the early myths. General Allenby miscalculated when he promised Prime Minister David Lloyd George that after liberating Jerusalem he

could quickly push Djamal Pasha's Fourth Army out of Syria–
Palestine and send troops back to France in time for the next
offensive in the spring of 1918. It turned out that the Ottomans
did not ask for an armistice and surrender until days before the
November 11 peace was declared in Europe between the Allies
and other Central Powers.

During those final months, both the Three Pashas and the
leaders of the Yishuv and *Ha-Shomer* had their own reasons to
dismiss the impact of Sarah and NILI on the inevitable Allied
victory in the Middle Eastern theater. In Zichron Ya'akov a cur-
tain of silence descended over Sarah's heroism and final betrayal.
The presence of Zvi Aaronsohn and the crippled Ephraim in
their midst could be neither ignored nor fully acknowledged.
The NILI agents who had been imprisoned were quietly set free
as Allenby's army drew close to Damascus and Turkish officials
began to flee to sanctuary elsewhere.

Once the war shifted to the struggle over the peace, other
myths began to surface. The diplomatic contest waged at the
Paris Peace Conference of 1919 featured a bitter argument over
who had better claim to parts of the Ottoman Empire coveted
by the victors. Sarah's two brothers, Aaron and Alexander, traveled between London and New York, where they were caught
up in postwar debate between President Wilson and Prime Minister Lloyd George over the duplicitous promises made to various Arab and Jewish leaders about their future roles in what was
going to be London's mandated rule over Palestine and Arabia.

The Arabists and the pro-Zionists in the military staff and
political ministries strengthened their cases by arguing about
whether the Jewish spies in Palestine or the Arab insurgents
had contributed most to the victory. William Ormsby-Gore
and Wyndham Deedes, and even General Allenby, publicly

credited Sarah and NILI with providing the crucial intelligence that led to the triumph. But their praise was more focused on devoted Aaron, who was still alive; Sarah was treated as a tragic but minor figure. The Arabists turned to the already celebrated T.E. Lawrence.

Aaron remained strangely muted when confronting his sister's fate. He had not learned of her death from the British until January, when he had gone from London to America to meet with Zionists there. He never returned to the Middle East. Instead, he made an uncomfortable truce with Chaim Weizmann and served as his aide at the Paris Peace Conference talks—where he clashed with the delegation headed by Sharif Hussein in his robes and T.E. Lawrence, who still wore a *keffiyeh* headdress over his officer's uniform.

Unhappy fates awaited Aaron and Alexander. In May 1919, Aaron was on his way back to the Paris conference from London via a Royal Flying Corps airplane when the aircraft crashed off the French coast, killing him and the pilot. Widespread rumors that the crash was due to official sabotage continue to circulate without resolution. Alexander was placated with military promotions and a Distinguished Service Order medal. The undeserved rewards pushed the already self-centered Alexander into a kind of delusion. He avoided returning very often to postwar Palestine. Instead he set himself up as an expert on the region and keeper of the NILI memory in both London and America. He actively promoted book and film projects that never materialized, and prospered for a time after marrying an heiress to a fortune founded on popular soap products. After a life of idleness, he died in 1948.

Sarah's other surviving relatives lived on in uneasy obscurity in Zichron Ya'akov. Zvi lived only until 1921 with the injuries inflicted on him; Shmuel died in 1950. Rivka returned from

America and cared for Ephraim in the house on Founders Street until his death in 1939. She lived on, unmarried, keeping a tight control over the large collection of Aaron's diaries, notebooks, and correspondence, which she selectively censored and then turned over to the Beit Aaronsohn–NILI Museum that was set up in the compound. She lived until 1981. The four women who were accused of betraying Sarah and shrieking at her as she went to her death all suffered and soon died painful and troubled deaths.

Rough justice also was meted out to Sarah's and NILI's Ottoman enemies after the war. All three of the Pashas fled prosecution by the reformists who seized control of what would become the new republic of Turkey. But they found no sanctuary. Assassins for the Armenian separatist movement tracked down Talaat Pasha in Berlin in 1921 and killed him. Djamal Pasha managed to become a military adviser to the rulers of Afghanistan who were waging a war with the new Soviet Union. In 1922, he was sent to Tbilisi, the capital of Georgia, for truce talks with the Soviets and was shot there—again by revenging Armenians. That same year, Enver Pasha was killed in battle leading a Muslim rebellion against the Soviets.

Only Aziz Bek, the head of the Ottoman counterespionage service, managed to survive. At the war's end he fled to Switzerland along with other Ottoman officials who feared prosecution. But after three years he returned to Turkey and spent two decades in a series of high offices in the new government of Kemal Ataturk. In the 1930s he published two memoirs in which he added to the layers of myth by alleging fanciful meetings with Sarah and describing a mutual attraction between them. He was never prosecuted for his oppression of either the Arabs or the Jews.

The most persistent myth of course is that of an ambivalent T.E. Lawrence and, tantalizingly, about his love for Sarah Aaronsohn. For the rest of his life until his death in 1935, Lawrence continued to shed identities and don new ones in search of the happiness that eluded him. He had plenty of help along the way.

British officialdom happily seized on the image of the daring English soldier-adventurer dashing across desert sands with his loyal band of Arab princes—part spymaster, part military genius. The government needed heroes once the horrible reality of the war began to sink into the public consciousness, and Lawrence was made to order.

He became a truly international celebrity thanks to an American showman-political operative named Lowell Thomas, who took a series of photographs and motion pictures of Lawrence during the war and attracted huge audiences in lecture halls across America. Thomas, with Lawrence at first a willing participant, shamelessly inflated the myth after the war with outlandish photographs of Lawrence in exotic Arab costumes. He used the images to illustrate a stream of books and articles that perpetuated fanciful fables of Lawrence as a master of disguise and daring, wandering at will behind Turkish lines and turning the tide of the Middle East campaign while heading his Arab band.

At the start, Lawrence took part in this charade. His government lavished medals and promotions on him. He became Colonel Lawrence and was feted everywhere including Buckingham Palace. He added to his own luster by publishing in 1926 the international best-selling memoir *Seven Pillars of Wisdom*—which had, by his own later admission, a number of embellishments included within its often impenetrable mix of memoir and philosophy.

Some of the fabrications later refuted, such as the victory at Aqaba and his capture and sexual torture at the hands of the Turks, found their way into the Hollywood film version of his legend. Among the persistent and dubious parts of the Lawrence myth are the allegations of his homosexuality and its impact on the rival myth of his love for Sarah Aaronsohn.

One of the more spurious assertions is that Lawrence's dedication of *Seven Pillars of Wisdom* "to S.A." refers to an Arab peasant boy named Dahoum, who was his servant and supposed lover during his archaeological work at Carchemish. Just to think what Leonard Woolley or D.G. Hogarth would have made of such behavior, let alone whether a confirmed Edwardian English gentleman as Lawrence remained all his life, would countenance such behavior, is to see it for the nonsense it is.

The absurdity is all the more ludicrous given the cultural evolution of progressive attitudes on gender identity and sexual relations that exist today. Yet the wrangle over whether Lawrence was or was not an active homosexual continues to produce a steady outpouring of books and articles. There is even an online Dutch website devoted to a detailed examination of the conflicting theories.

It is telling that contemporaries of Lawrence who were skeptics and some outright foes such as Colonel (later General) Walter Gribbon and Richard Meinertzhagen, who did conduct spy raids behind Turkish lines, dismissed such a notion. Meinertzhagen brought criticism down on himself by publicly declaring, "Lawrence never commanded anything but a looting rabble of murderous Arabs, he took part in no military operations and his desert exploits had not the slightest bearing on Allenby's campaign. In his own words his was a 'side-show of a side-show. . . . ' I probably knew Lawrence better than any living man. . . . I believe I was the only one of his friends to whom he confided that he was a 'complete fraud.'" Yet he, Leonard Woolley, and others present during his archaeological and wartime lives later publicly refuted the homosexuality myth.

It is probably more accurate to describe Lawrence's exploits in the desert as both brave and important, if not crucial, to Allenby's victory. More than the British liaison officers with other tribes, he managed a fragile coalition of tribal forces that forced the Turks to divert large numbers of troops away from the Gaza–Beersheba front. That should be glory enough for any man.

As for Lawrence himself, his sad search for a better identity quite plausibly could have led him to adopt part of Sarah Aaronsohn's own very real heroism for himself. He gradually wearied of the Lawrence of Arabia image and shed it just as he had others before. Part of this was no doubt due to his government's dismissal of the Arab cause and his dismay at how the Arabs had proved themselves unable to achieve unity. He resigned his army rank, dropped out of sight, and adopted a new name altogether. After being dismissed as an enlisted man in the army, he found a new enthusiasm in the romantic future that aviation promised in the 1920s. He became Aircraftman T.E. Shaw and a mechanic in the Royal Flying Corps.

As for the woman he never met but clearly admired, his conversation and disclosure to Douglas Duff in a Dorset village store in the 1930s can plausibly be read as yet another of his attempts to appropriate something of Sarah's very real heroism to bolster his own fragile self-esteem. A related motive could be that Lawrence late in life came to a sense of guilt in part because of the way the Arabists at the Savoy headquarters had hampered—or even subverted—what Sarah and NILI were laboring in constant danger to achieve.

So Lawrence's poem can be taken as a form of apology to Sarah as much as an attempt to attach himself to her legend. He could claim, "I loved you, so I drew these tides of men into my hands and wrote my will across the sky in stars to earn you

Freedom." But even with that claim, he forced himself to admit in the final stanzas that his attempt to build her a "fit monument" ended up shattered and unfinished.

Sarah Aaronsohn's legend continues to grow. Her dream of *Eretz Israel* is a reality. It is an imperfect one, to be sure. The Jewish–Arab comity that was briefly possible seems an unlikely prospect these days.

Visitors to the Beit Aaronsohn–NILI Museum, established in Zichron Ya'akov in 1956, should find inspiration in the life and heroic deeds of Sarah and her family. Sarah's courage and leadership made her a woman ahead of her time. One hopes she will serve as an inspiration to future leaders rather than merely a historic figure whom Israeli schoolchildren honor when they visit her grave in the now-prosperous suburb of Haifa that is Zichron Ya'akov.

POSTSCRIPT

Lawrence of Arabia (ca. 1917)

From the frontispiece of his privately printed edition of *Seven Pillars of Wisdom* by T.E. Lawrence, 1926:

To S.A.

I loved you, so I drew these tides of men into my hands
And wrote my will across the sky in stars
To earn you Freedom, the seven pillared worthy house
That your eyes might be shining for me
When we came.
Death seemed thy servant on the road, till we were near
And saw you waiting;

When you smiled, and in sorrowful envy he outran me
    And took you apart: into his quietness.
Love, the way-weary, grasped to your body, our brief wage
    Ours for the moment
Before earth's soft hand explored your shape, and the blind
    Worms grew fat upon your substance.
Men prayed me that I set out work, the inviolate house,
    As a memory of you.
But for fit monument I shattered it, unfinished and now
The little things creep out to patch themselves hovels
        In the marred shadow
        Of your gift.

An Explanation

Douglas Duff was at Thear's Garage in the Dorset village of Bridport on a spring day in 1935 when he met the fabled T.E. Lawrence.

Duff had been a knockabout adventurer who for some years had been the prolific writer of thrilling adventure stories of the kind favored by British schoolboys as "ripping yarns." His latest book had been set in the Middle East, where he had been chief of Jerusalem's notorious Palestine Police that enforced British rule in that volatile region after World War I. He certainly would have known Lawrence of Arabia on sight. More than twenty years later in a letter footnoted in an obscure intelligence study, he recalled:

> *That morning I was filling my petrol tank at the garage,*
> *when a large Brough Superior motorcycle roared up and I*
> *saw, without him seeing me, that it was Lawrence. I knew*
> *he hated recognition, and made none, but I heard him ask*

the pump attendant who I was and my name was given. Then Lawrence, a small man, came up and spoke in the strange way he had of using soldierly language, very soldierly. He asked me if I had written a recent book on Palestine which I had dedicated to Sarah Aaronsohn. I was very flattered to think he had read my work and said so. The conversation went like this (without hoping to be verbatim):

L: *So you know who I am?*
Me: *I do. Col. Lawrence, of course.*
L: *Shaw's my name and I'm no _____ colonel.*
Me: *I beg your pardon, I'm afraid you will always be Lawrence in my mind. I apologize for saying so aloud.*
L: *Did you know Sarah Aaronsohn while she was alive?*
Me: *I'm very sorry that I did not. I'd have given my right arm to have done so.*
L: *Why?*
Me: *Good Lord, man, if there was a Joan of Arc in our days, it was Sarah!*
L: *Strange we two men should be here in this little town, both of us with a book dedicated to her, without either of us having seen her alive.*
Me: *Why, judging by that sonnet of yours I was sure she and you were partners in the old days.*
L: *We were—but without meeting.*

Later in the conversation, Lawrence added, "If she had a man for a husband, she might have been the leader of a Hebrew return with glory. It must have been hell to be married to her when one was unable to appreciate her."

Three months later, on a rural lane near his cottage at Clouds

Hill, Lawrence was struck by a black sedan that zx0 said had four men as passengers. The car never stopped. Lawrence died a day later without regaining consciousness, and the speculation that he was murdered lingers to this day.

NOTES

Prologue

Alexander Aaronsohn, *Sarah, The Flame of NILI* (unpublished manuscript provided by the Beit Aaronsohn–NILI Museum, Zichron Ya'akov, Israel).

Anita Engle, *The NILI Spies* (London: Frank Cass Publishers, 1959), 208–229.

Shmuel Katz, *The Aaronsohn Saga* (Jerusalem: Green Publishing House, 2000), 263–276.

Ida Cowen and Irene Gunther, *A Spy for Freedom* (New York: Lodestar Books, 1984), 141–154.

Hillel Halkin, *A Strange Death* (New York: Public Affairs, 2005), 172–187.

Chapter One: Who Was Sarah Aaronsohn?

Patricia Goldstone, *Aaronsohn's Maps* (New York: Harcourt, 2007), 12–39.

Ronald Florence, *Lawrence and Aaronsohn: T.E. Lawrence, Aaron Aaronsohn, and the Seeds of the Arab–Israeli Conflict* (New York: Penguin, 2007), 30–52.

Chapter Two: Friends in America

Katz, 13–19.

David Fairchild, *The World Was My Garden: Travels of a Plant Explorer* (New York: Charles Scribner's Sons, 1938), 47–62.

Engle, 28–29.

Chapter Three: The Three Pashas

Richard C. Hall, *The Balkan Wars 1912–1913: Prelude to the First World War* (London: Routledge, 2000), 1–24.

Eugene Rogan, *The Fall of the Ottomans: The Great War in the Middle East* (New York: Basic Books, 2015), 1–28.

Edmond Taylor, *The Fall of the Dynasties: The Collapse of the Old Order, 1905–1922* (New York: Doubleday, 1962), 97–122.

DanielYergin, *The Prize:The Epic Quest for Oil, Money and Power* (NewYork: Simon & Schuster, 1991), 173–181.

Chapter Four: Love and War
Engle, 32–39.
Katz, 75–90.
Cowen and Gunther, 17–32.
James Srodes, *On Dupont Circle: Franklin and Eleanor Roosevelt and the Progressives Who Shaped Our World* (Berkeley, CA: Counterpoint, 2013), 17–49.

Chapter Five: Plagues of War and Locusts
Goldstone, 106–107, 112–113.
Katz, 152–185.
Walter Gribbon, Brigadier, *Agents of Empire:Anglo–Zionist Intelligence Operations 1915–1919* (London: Brassey's, 1995), 89–100.
Aaronsohn, 22–40.
Alexander Aaronsohn, *With the Turks in Palestine* (New York: Houghton, Mifflin, 1916), 49–69.
Cohen and Gunther, 35–41.
Ibid., 44.
Katz, 48–61.
Gribbon, 93–124.
British National Archives Foreign Office and War Office files, FO371, FO157.
Goldstone, 91–101.

Chapter Six: Success and Setback
Katz, 101–132.
Cohen and Gunther, 33–65.
Aaronsohn, *Sarah, the Flame of NILI,* 27–29, 33–42.
Engle, 51–76.
Gribbon, translations from Aaron Aaronsohn's diaries, 223–306.

Chapter Seven: Sarah Takes Command
Gribbon, 122–173.
British National Archives War Office Files,WO 157/689.
Imperial War Museum File, Box 69/48/3; Box 69/48/4; Box 6 File39/4. See also, FO 371/471, FO 371/3057/3058.

Katz, 5–9.

Anthony Sattin, *The Young T.E. Lawrence* (New York: Norton, 2014), 133–157.

Cohen and Gunther, 2; 75–79.

Aaronsohn, *Sarah, the Flame of NILI*, 23.

Sarah Aaronsohn, translation, Beit Aaronsohn Archives. Also, Goldstone, 228.

Ibid.

Chapter Eight: Sarah Gets Her Orders and NILI Gets Its Name

Gribbon, quotes from Aaron Aaronsohn's diaries, 226–239. Copies of the diaries, which he wrote in French, are housed both at the British National Archives and at the Beit Aaronsohn–NILI Museum. Aaron's disdain for Lawrence only intensified with time. On August 12, 1917 he recorded, "I had a chat with Capt. Lawrence this morning. Our interview was devoid of amenity. He has been too successful at an early age—and is infatuated with himself. He gave me a lesson on our colonies—the mentality of the people—the feelings of the Arabs, etc., etc. As I was listening to him I could almost imagine that I was attending a conference by a scientific, anti-Semitic Prussian speaking English. . . . One would gather from the above interview that nothing can be done in Judea and Samaria where Faisal will never gain access. . . . But Lawrence will conduct his investigation by his own methods in order to learn of the mentality of the Jews (there). . . . If they are in favor of the Arabs they shall be spared, otherwise they shall have their throats cut. He is still at the age where people do not doubt themselves—happy young man! He is plainly hostile to us. He must be of a missionary breed." Gribbon, 289.

Katz, 225–240.

Florence, 264–267.

Goldstone, 154–163.

Katz, 116.

Chapter Nine: Sarah and NILI Make a Difference

Goldstone, 170.

Katz, 272–273, quoting testimony from Dr. Hillel Yaffe and Rivka Lishansky.

Ibid., 234. The letter is in the Beit Aaronsohn–NILI Museum, Zichron Ya'akov, Israel.

Chapter Ten: The Net Closes

Gribbon, 310–311. In an appendix, Gribbon provides the EMSIB list of the "A Organization" members naming twenty-three "active" members who "were actually doing the work, traveling about the country, collecting data, meeting the trawlers, etc." Also named are twelve other "passive" members and two others, Liova Schneersohn and Raphael Aboulafia, who sailed on the *Managem* during its twice-monthly visits to Athlit during 1917. Schneersohn was the courier who went ashore each time, while Aboulafia translated the intelligence documents from Hebrew to English on the return voyages so they would be immediately put to use when they reached Port Said.

Katz, 225–240.

Florence, 264–267.

Goldstone, 154–163.

Katz, 116.

Ibid., 227.

Ibid., 228.

Aaron Aaronsohn, Diaries, August 12, 1917. Quoted in Gribbon, 288–289.

British National Archives, Box 23G, FO141/803 EMSIB briefing on Beirut minefields and troop movements, ". . . the best we have received this year." Also, Monthly Intelligence Summaries and War Diary briefings: WO157/715/18, WO157/713, and WO159/718, reference to "Our Syrian Organization." Translated by Sophie Crochet.

Epilogue: Myth versus History

Maarten Schild, *T.E. Lawrence, Before and After Arabia* (www.maartenschild.com).

Richard Meinertzhagen, Lt. Col., *Middle East Diary* (London: Cresset Press, 1959), 43–46. Also, Katz, 339.

Duff's anecdote has been widely reprinted but with conflicting interpretations. For example, two Israeli historians agree that Lawrence probably did not have a physical romance with Sarah but disagree whether his poem is dedicated to her. Yigal Sheffy, in a note in the *British Intelligence and Security Journal*, Vol. 4, 1990 cites it as evidence that Lawrence had loved her. Anita Engle, in her earlier book, *The NILI Spies*, argues to the contrary. No one, however, disputes Duff's recollection of the conversation. See also Imperial War Museum files on Lawrence Box 6, file 6/384D Lawrence's poem as edited by Robert Graves. File 6/389D, a fifteen-page account of the identity of Sarah in the poem by Somerset de Chair.

Acknowledgments

I must mention with special gratitude those who were a great help along the way. Daniel C. W. Wilson, a talented British historian, proved an indefatigable and enthusiastic researcher at the various military and intelligence files at the British National Archives at Kew, at the Imperial War Museum in London and elsewhere. Dr. Marion Freudenthal, the archivist at the Beit Aaronsohn–NILI Museum in Zichron Ya'akov, Israel was extremely generous in providing documents and photographs that were essential to Sarah's story. Sophie Crochet of Swarthmore College put her bilingual skills to good use translating the correspondence between Sarah's brother Aaron Aaronsohn and Zionist leader Chaim Weizmann, which was in an arcane formal French. Eddie Friedmann was a wise guide to the culture of Zichron Ya'akov. Ronald Goldfarb, my literary adviser and friend, was a fount of insight and encouragement. Charlie Winton and the rest of the Counterpoint Press staff, as before, have been supportive at every step.

And for more decades that I care to count, my greatest gratitude and greater love belong to Cecile Srodes, the best copy editor, wife, and friend an undeserving man could wish for.

Index

*Page references for illustrations appear in **bold** type*

Printed in the United States
by Baker & Taylor Publisher Services